SENCO Leadership

Written by SENCOs for SENCOs and other school leaders, this book shares innovative, strategic and practical whole-school developments that have been trialed and reviewed through research with colleagues, students and families.

Each chapter is written by an experienced SENCO school leader. Their accounts of the developments they carried out and the research evidence they collected to measure impact are presented accessibly and succinctly. These developments include:

- Preparing for Ofsted Inspection
- SEN policy and whole-school practice: what are staff doing and what do they know?
- Whole-school referral for SEND Support
- Capturing voices. Increasing all students' experience of belonging in school
- Exclusion: The impact of limited wider-life experiences

SENCO Leadership: Implementing Whole-School Practice is an indispensable resource for all SENCOs and other school leaders wanting to provide the best learning environment for their whole school community.

Gill Richards is Emeritus Professor of Special Education, Equity and Inclusion at Nottingham Trent University, UK.

Jane Starbuck is the Strategic Lead for School Support and Growth for The Community Inclusive Trust (CIT).

A View into the Classroom
Series edited by Gill Richards

A View into the Classroom is a unique series, written by and for education practitioners. Supported throughout with real-life case studies of success, books in this series offer easy access to practical school-based education research for a wide range of teachers who want to understand more about issues that interest and challenge them. With the current focus on 'evidence-based practice' in education settings, all teachers increasingly need to become 'research literate', so these accounts will provide valuable insight for any teacher about manageable research processes that can be incorporated into their own professional activities to become more effective in the classroom, with greater impact on their students.

Innovative School Leadership
Transforming Practices
Gill Richards and Chris Wheatley

SENCO Leadership
Implementing Whole-School Practice
Gill Richards and Jane Starbuck

Effective Interventions and Strategies for Pupils with SEND
Using Evidence-Based Methods for Maximum Impact
Gill Richards and Jane Starbuck

For more information about this series, please visit: https://www.routledge.com/A-View-into-the-Classroom/book-series/VCLSRM

SENCO Leadership

Implementing Whole-School Practice

Edited by Gill Richards and Jane Starbuck

Routledge
Taylor & Francis Group

LONDON AND NEW YORK

First edition published 2025
by Routledge
4 Park Square, Milton Park, Abingdon, Oxon, OX14 4RN

and by Routledge
605 Third Avenue, New York, NY 10158

Routledge is an imprint of the Taylor & Francis Group, an informa business

© 2025 selection and editorial matter, Gill Richards and
Jane Starbuck; individual chapters, the contributors

The right of Gill Richards and Jane Starbuck to be identified
as the authors of the editorial material, and of the authors for
their individual chapters, has been asserted in accordance with
sections 77 and 78 of the Copyright, Designs and Patents Act 1988.

British Library Cataloguing-in-Publication Data
A catalogue record for this book is available from the British Library

Library of Congress Cataloging-in-Publication Data
Names: Richards, Gill, editor. | Starbuck, Jane, editor.
Title: SENCO leadership : implementing whole-school
    practice / Edited by Gill Richards and Jane Starbuck.
Description: First edition. | Abingdon, Oxon ; New York,
    NY : Routledge, 2025. | Series: A view into the classroom:
    teachers' research into effective practice | Includes
    bibliographical references and index.
Identifiers: LCCN 2024025983 (print) | LCCN 2024025984
    (ebook) | ISBN 9781032738932 (hardback) | ISBN 9781032738901
    (paperback) | ISBN 9781003466550 (ebook)
Subjects: LCSH: School management and organization. | Classroom
    management. | Problem children—Behavior modification. |
    Belonging (Social psychology) | School improvement programs.
Classification: LCC LB2805 .S5164 2025 (print) | LCC LB2805
    (ebook) | DDC 370.15/8—dc23/eng/20240716
LC record available at https://lccn.loc.gov/2024025983
LC ebook record available at https://lccn.loc.gov/2024025984

ISBN: 978-1-032-73893-2 (hbk)
ISBN: 978-1-032-73890-1 (pbk)
ISBN: 978-1-003-46655-0 (ebk)

DOI: 10.4324/9781003466550

Typeset in Sabon
by Apex CoVantage, LLC

Contents

Acknowledgements

We would like to thank the contributing SENCO leaders for sharing their experiences of implementing whole-school change in their schools. We hope their work will inspire other SENCOs and school leaders to implement strategic developments across their school that will benefit all students.

We would like to thank the headteachers for supporting the projects included within this book and the teachers, students and wider school staff for their valuable contributions.

We would like to thank Alison Foyle (Senior Publisher) for her encouragement of our original new venture with teachers' research that has now provided the opportunity for over 40 teacher authors to share their learning within four books in this series. We are also very grateful to the team at Routledge for their support in ensuring that our book was ready for publication.

Author biographies

Editors

Gill Richards taught for 21 years in schools and further education, then in universities, becoming Professor of Special Education, Equity and Inclusion. She has been a project leader for UK government-funded SEND projects with teachers and SENCOs in schools, and a European Erasmus project about behaviour in Greece. Her most recent research work includes a NCTL nationally funded project on lessening teachers' workload, a DfE-funded project with Secondary SENCOs, and an eight-year study of the aspirations and achievements of girls living in an area of severe deprivation. She currently teaches SENCOs on the mandatory award, and postgraduate teacher apprentices about action research. She also supports schools with developing their own research culture.

Jane Starbuck is the Strategic Lead for School Support and Growth for The Community Inclusive Trust (CIT). She works with schools in a school development capacity and also leads on creating a coordinated and consistent approach to growing the MAT. Jane was a SENCO and primary school Head Teacher and the Strategic Leader for Inclusion of a large partnership of schools. More recently, she worked for Nottinghamshire County Council as a SEND Adviser. She is also the Deputy Regional Leader for East Midlands, South Yorkshire and Humber for Whole School SEND. Jane has a particular interest in developing a strategy-based approach to SEND provision in schools. She has established effective collaborations between schools to develop specialist provision, alternative provision, training and sharing resources. Jane is also a lecturer on the National SENCO Award for Nottingham Trent University.

Authors

Michaela Brown has been a teacher since 1998 after qualifying with a B.Ed. and Diploma in Special Needs. She has worked in five different primary schools, teaching through the entire primary phase. She has had many roles in her career – phase leader, curriculum lead and Advanced Skills Teacher leading a computing network for a Trust and supporting teachers with their practice. She has also delivered units on their SCITT programme and completed training to become facilitator for the Creative Teacher programme. Michaela is currently Deputy Head, SENCO, Pastoral Team Lead and Designated Safeguarding Lead at one of the largest primary schools in their county. She has been in her deputy role for seven years and has returned to her passion of special educational needs.

Emma Butler has been an English teacher in secondary schools since 2013 and has worked in both mainstream settings and specialist provisions. She has taught across all key stages and year groups from Years 7 to 13. Her time in a specialist provision inspired her to take the knowledge and experience back into mainstream and she qualified as a SENCO in 2021 to complement her role of Assistant Headteacher. More recently, Emma has been appointed as a Deputy Headteacher, responsible for Pastoral and Inclusion: she is now able to have a more influential voice to support all students in school.

Jemma Cotton has been a primary school teacher since 2014, specialising in special educational needs. She has worked in schools in significantly deprived areas. She completed the NPQML in 2017, focusing on language development, then became Early Years Lead and Designated Teacher for Looked After Children in 2018. In 2019, she took on the roles of Designated Safeguarding Lead and Special Educational Needs Co-ordinator. Completing the NPQSL in 2023, she focused on subject knowledge and assessment for learning. Currently, Jemma is undergoing Senior Mental Health lead training, while supporting other schools in their Early Years and Special Needs provision.

Eleanor Dorrington has been a teacher since 2014 and currently works at an inner-city primary school in the East Midlands. She has worked in two different local authorities and taught across all phases, predominantly in upper Key Stage Two. In 2016, she completed a Masters' degree in Psychology at the University of

Nottingham with the ambition to train as an Educational Psychologist. Eleanor has been the SENDCo at her current school since 2018 and is part of the senior management team. She has also supported staff in various schools within the multi-academy trust where she works and led the MAT SENDCo network.

Lauren Farrar has been a primary school teacher since 2015 and has taught across the whole of Key Stage 2, predominately in Years 5 and 6. She has held many subject leadership roles throughout the years, including English, Design and Technology and Geography. She has been a mentor to student teachers who have been training in her school, guiding and supporting these future teachers at the start of their careers. Lauren has completed her NPQSL and is on the Senior Leadership Team. Her current roles are class teacher in a mixed Year 5 and 6 class, school SENCo and Upper Key Stage 2 leader. She has also recently taken a lead on Pupil Premium in her school.

Katie Hawksley has been a SENDCo since January 2024, following two years as Assistant SENDCo at the same school. After finishing her English and History degree at the University of Sheffield in 2019, Katie went on to complete a PGCE and intended to teach English. Initially, she took a position as a pastoral manager before finding her passion for SEND and moving to work as a literacy teaching assistant and then becoming Assistant SENDCo later that academic year. Katie is currently completing the National Award for SEN Coordination.

Emma Haywood graduated with a BA Hons with QTS degree in 2000 and has been an educator ever since. She has taught all primary ages, but has predominantly worked within Early Years. In 2013 Emma became a primary Headteacher following her completion of the NPQH, and so understands the successes, as well as the challenges this role can bring. Her latest position as a Headteacher and SENCo of a nursery school has strengthened her additional role as a Director of Initial Teacher Training, supporting the teachers of the future. In recent years Emma has been working alongside the NCB and EEF to support research projects for Early Years practitioners.

Vanessa Mehta has been a secondary school teacher since 1994, working in three different schools, primarily as a Science and PSHE teacher. Alongside this, she has worked for PiXL for five years producing character resources for schools, supporting schools nationally and presenting at the PiXL conferences. Having held numerous leadership roles, including Head of Science, Assistant Head and Deputy Head, her current role is as Deputy Head with a responsibility for the strategic lead of safeguarding and SEND. Vanessa has achieved the National Award for SEN Co-ordination and the NPQH qualification for Headteachers. Her passion is ensuring equality for all.

Tom Voice has held a variety of middle and senior leadership roles. He has been a SENCO in a secondary school in the East Midlands for over nine years. Previously, he worked one day a week across primary schools, supporting students with special educational needs be successful throughout their education. He has represented schools within local authority improvement boards, working in partnership with health and social care. Currently he is seconded to lead on the provision for students with additional needs across a multi-academy trust for two days a week, whilst holding the role of Assistant Headteacher for Inclusion.

Sue Winton has a background in primary education and was a Headteacher for 13 years. She worked for Nottinghamshire Children's Services designing and facilitating events for Headteachers and Governing Bodies, managing the changes brought about by government policy. She was involved in design and delivery of the NPQs for Inspiring Leaders and the National College of School Leadership. She is a certified coach and works with Headteachers, Finance and HR Directors, Social Care leaders, Aspirant Directors of Children's Services and business leaders. Sue has facilitated the Leadership part of the SENCO Award at Nottingham Trent University for the last eight years.

Introduction

Jane Starbuck, Sue Winton and Gill Richards

SEND is everybody's business

This book is an incredibly important resource for all school leaders. It identifies the impact a SENCO can have across a school when they are empowered to do so and are recognised as a leader of education. Each chapter identifies practical ways in which SENCOs can work and become effective leaders – from the steps and actions to take in the first 100 days of taking up the role to working in collaboration with other colleagues to develop an inclusive environment that ensures high-quality adaptive teaching for all. The authors identify how important it is for SENCOs to work in partnership with all teams in school to develop appropriate and proactive support for students who are vulnerable or high profile. Alongside this they emphasise the need for SENCOs to be able to develop effective working partnerships with any available expertise within their locality.

SENCOs are often the unsung heroes or 'go to' for families and students when they are struggling with school systems. This book identifies the importance of developing systems and processes to be able to capture 'voice' and provide a range of ways for students to communicate their views on how these impact on their lives.

Provided with adequate time, support and status, SENCOs can create partnerships and provision in school that impact not just on students with SEND but on the quality of teaching and learning, effective pastoral support and systems, along with ensuring that any additional adults impact positively on learning and progress. The most successful schools provide SENCOs with more professional freedom to develop provision to meet the needs of the most

DOI: 10.4324/9781003466550-1

vulnerable students in school, to work alongside teachers to build understanding and confidence in their own practice, and to create systems and processes that highlight that SEND is everybody's responsibility.

The SENCO is one of the few leaders in school who are responsible for a considerable budget along with ensuring a school meets its statutory responsibilities in terms of EHCPs, reasonable adjustments and meeting need. So, as with any other leader in school, SENCOs need to have the opportunity to monitor the impact of the support they have co-ordinated and to be able to feed this back, as a leader, to SLT and governors. Their work impacts every curriculum area and classroom. When the school leadership recognise the need to prioritise SEND and build systems into whole-school processes, then teachers become confident in adapting practice and students are able to thrive.

I believe every headteacher should read this book to see how a group of SENCOs, when provided with the support, opportunity and time, have been able to influence and develop so many practices across their schools. It is then the challenge for those headteachers to engage in conversations and reflection so that they can identify what it is they must do to enable and empower SENCOs to become effective strategic leaders in their own settings.

Jane Starbuck

SENCO leadership: making an impact

I have worked directly with SENCO leaders over the past ten years studying for their SENCO qualification and I have noticed a pattern emerging around their leadership and management. I have highlighted three areas where SENCOs and other leaders I have coached have had a high impact.

1. **Knowing what is important** to you as SENCO leader. This helps shape your strategy for growth and helps with alignment when working with others.
2. **Knowing your leadership style and developing others.** This relies on you being open to feedback and being willing to make changes to enable others to grow.
3. **Recognising the importance of all communication.** It can be a driver for change, it can help build trust, but, unattended, can be the reason things go wrong.

Context is key and I realise that my following suggestions will not suit every setting, but you might find it helpful take note of the principles and adapt them for yourself. Courageous leaders keep an open mind, they look for new opportunities and often create something better. You are already a courageous leader by choosing to become a SENCO!

Knowing what is important

As SENCO leader, you can influence the thoughts, feelings, and behaviours of others. Ask your stakeholders the following questions to create an aligned vision for the future and to drive ongoing collaboration: Who are we? Why are we here? What is specifically important to this area of our work? *To do this, you might find Tool 1 useful.

Tool 1: Alignment. Extract key words from stakeholders' answers (for example, 'Inclusion') and give everyone a Post-it note, asking them to:

- Individually define 'Why is inclusion important?' and then share/compare with others.
- Form small groups and determine a group definition.
- Repeat the process until they have one agreed, whole-group definition.
- Explore what it would mean in day-to-day practice, capturing examples and creating guiding principles.

When decisions are required, never assume others think like you, *check understanding.*

Knowing your leadership style and developing others

Understanding your own style of leadership and how to develop others is important. It can help to recall those leaders you most admire and those you feel frustrated by. What exactly it is about them that influences your thoughts and behaviours? Also, try reflecting on the following questions:

- What kind of leader do you want to be and what do you want to be known for?
- If others talked about you, what would you want them to be saying?

- What are your strengths and areas for growth?
- What needs developing in others?

Avoid the 'tell syndrome'

In 'time poor' situations it is easy to slip into autocratic 'TELL syndrome'. This can be triggered by you feeling you have to be the fountain of all knowledge. Someone asks a question, and you tell them the answer. You may slip into 'telling' in meetings, to save time, or to 'help' people by giving lists of instructions. By operating like this you are creating a dependency culture, you are doing all the thinking and depriving others of that skill. If it becomes habitual, others around you will turn off, become resentful, believe their thoughts and ideas are not valued.

Develop an open questioning approach to enable others to learn and grow – consider: What are your thoughts and ideas? Where are the risks? When is the deadline? Who else could help?

Recognising the importance of all communication

All communication matters, but as a SENCO leader three areas of communication are particularly important.

How you make people feel

As SENCO you are in the spotlight delivering a very important service through others. You will most likely be judged on 'how you make people feel'. Before you plan any 'WHAT's,' spend time considering 'WHY' what you are proposing is important, to ensure engagement and 'buy -in', and then 'HOW' you partner with others to achieve that collective focus – 'We-Centric' leadership. *Consider using Tool 2 to create a collaborative approach.

Tool 2: Working collaboratively. Reflect with others – what is 'Working Well' and 'What is Not Working So Well', and Why? Use the responses to jointly identify ideas/suggestions for solutions, resources and agreed actions with time scales for check-ins/monitoring.

What are people 'Thinking, Feeling and Saying' about you? Show that you care, listen, and build relationships based on TRUST: Transparency, Relationships, Understanding, Shared success, Truth telling. You can achieve this in many ways by noticing the small important things and acknowledging effort. Also, be visible, model what you want to see, check yourself for positive body language. Always prepare yourself for meetings. Consider how you want to be received by others and make your messages clear and concise, matching your messaging to your audience; remember timing is key. Decide on your purpose – inform, influence, involve.

When managing, remember your own well-being by resisting back-to-back appointments, allocating time for planning, and taking regular breaks. Use an electronic diary, giving others access *after* you have allocated time for your own tasks and allocated available slots for last-minute meeting requests. Keep people up to date, use the collaborative tool (Tool 2) as the basis of your agenda and feedback for all meetings.

As a member of the senior leadership team (if you are not, get on it!)

Make sure you use your voice and contribute regularly. Study the agenda in advance, decide where you can make a valid contribution – speak confidently and use research where possible to back up your suggestions and ideas. Think carefully about the outcomes you are seeking. Take every opportunity to further them. Get good at noticing and asking open questions. Stay focused, listen carefully to others, be highly curious.

Navigating tricky or difficult conversations

SENCOs experience many situations where they have to manage challenging conversations. If you find these difficult or not as productive as you would like, try asking yourself:

- What kind of conversations do you find difficult?
- What is inhibiting you having these conversations? Speak to others about this.
- If I say 'yes' to this, what am I saying 'no' to?

Use your answers to these to help you plan more successful strategies. For example, when someone asks to see you, acknowledge its importance, allocate time as soon as possible. *Always* give yourself time to plan your approach and response. You also might find Tool 3 useful.

Tool 3: WIN. Having a simple tool to provide a framework for difficult conversations provides the structure for agreed next steps:

> **W** – What happened? Invite both parties to tell the story from their own perspective.
> **I** – Impact. Both parties reflect on the 'So What?' (e.g. 'The impact was . . .').
> **N** – Next steps. Now what we have agreed is . . . by . . . (next review).

These questions and tools will help SENCOs to engage others in a common purpose. Set the standards and expectations to ensure clarity, consistency and confidence in your offer to parents and families. Look for opportunities to join and connect the parts and create systems and processes to allow others to work at their best. Be a courageous leader!

Sue Winton

SENCO leadership: professional curiosity and evidence-based decisions

> High quality, evidence-based teaching is critical in ensuring that the special educational needs of pupils are not mis-identified when their difficulties may be due to poor classroom provision, as well as ensuring that the needs of those with SEN are met effectively.
>
> (DfE 2023: 54)

This DfE statement reflects the importance of the way in which SENCOs must be able to carry out their role. The earlier SEND review (DfE 2022) stated that *excellent* teaching was the 'bedrock' of strong provision for all pupils, especially for those with SEND, and that SENCOs should be *leaders* within their schools who shared expertise and guidance, while setting the *strategic* direction of day-to-day SEND provision.

Clearly, if SENCOs are to achieve this, they need to be in a position where they can work strategically and access (or generate) robust evidence to ensure that the specific needs of pupils with SEND are being accurately identified and met effectively. Three issues can impact this:

- SENCOs report nationally that they do not have sufficient time to carry out their role – their ability to work strategically is often overwhelmed by the demands of everyday provision and administration (Curran and Boddison 2021).

- SENCOs are often not on their school's senior leadership team, so they may lack the power required to impact the strategic direction of provision, especially when they are viewed by colleagues as 'specialist advisors' rather than leaders (Kay *et al.* 2022).

- SENCO responsibility can be viewed as primarily located within a 'Learning Support Team' rather than, as one SENCO recently described it, "You are leading SEN: your team is the whole school!"

SENCOs need to know – what is working, what isn't and why?

Professional curiosity

Do SENCOs always know what is happening in their school's SEND provision? I ask that not in any way to criticise, but because after working with SENCOs for over 20 years, they have told me time and again that there are situations that worry them: situations where provision doesn't seem to be working as it should or where students tell them things are different to what they have been told by staff.

Providing time and support for SENCOs to be strategic leaders is essential if schools are to ensure that every aspect of their provision is high quality *and* consistent. It doesn't matter what is in a school policy if *all* the staff aren't doing it, so SENCOs need to be in the position of knowing what is happening across the school and able to make changes if required.

From our work with SENCOs on the National Award and a recent project with Secondary SENCOs, Jane and I have consistently found that when given the opportunity to strategically investigate elements of whole-school practice, SENCOs were surprised by what they discovered – for example, three reported:

I discovered our school's interventions weren't being carried properly, or as often as they should. Now I audit this regularly and achievement has increased.

Students consistently identified the same staff who didn't 'get them' and meet their needs. My chance to do lesson observations supported this. The project revealed it is a bigger problem than I'd realised.

My student focus groups identified a group of LGBQT+ students who felt vulnerable in school.

It can be easy to assume that if policies are in place and interventions are set up, all is working smoothly – and this may well be the case. However, in all of the situations described previously, the SENCOs were able to respond quickly by implementing changes that significantly benefitted students, but they were clear – without being set a specific task of working strategically and allocated the time to do it, they would not have discovered these situations so quickly.

Using evidence to make strategic decisions about provision

'Evidence' comes in different forms and can be found in different places. SENCOs will find two sorts of evidence particularly useful:

1. Evidence of what is happening in school. Are relevant policies, practices and specialist interventions:
   a) working as they should for everyone, and if so, what is the measurable impact?
   b) not working, and if not, why not? For example, what specifically is preventing them from being successful and is this always the case?

2. Robust evidence of developments, new initiatives and research studies taking place (inter)nationally that would be useful to consider for school SEND practice.

When considering any kind of evidence, it is important to reflect on the quality of the source. Does what is being claimed stand up to scrutiny? For example:

a) Who was involved and what was the context? Is there any 'over-claiming' of results?
b) Why was the evidence collected, and was there any funding – could this have influenced what is being claimed?
c) Was evidence collected from everything/everywhere/everyone relevant? If it was just a selection, why? Was that made clear and might it have affected the results?

When reviewing school provision strategically, SENCOs may use whole-school numerical data (often viewed as 'hard data'), but this has limitations because it provides information of successes or problems, but not the reasons *why* these occur. SENCOs will gain a more robust understanding of situations by checking 'the story' behind 'hard data' through collecting additional information from surveys, interviews and focus groups with students, staff and families. This will help them understand 'why' and inform their *evidence-based* decision-making.

Benefits for students

Evidence-informed decisions are important. They can positively support student achievement, but also prevent the continued use of strategies where the cause of lack of progress may be placed on students rather than the quality (or inaccurate match to need) of the strategy, which increases their experiences of failure and creates staff frustration.

Every student has the right to experience successful learning, and all staff have a key role in providing this, so we need to get this right:

> As educators we must be proactive in seeking out the knowledge and skills to enable every one of our students to be successful learners. I believe that when one child fails to learn, it may have a small impact on a school, but it represents 100% failure for that child and is unacceptable.
>
> (Hattie 2016: 219)
> Gill Richards

This book

This book describes the work of SENCO leaders who investigated practice in their schools. They aim to share what they learned and, by explaining the processes they used, help readers understand how these can be replicated. It is recognised that these are all small-scale studies, and there is no intention to 'over-claim' any findings. Each SENCO wanted to demonstrate practical ways in which busy SENCOs and other teachers can collect evidence in school to benefit students' learning experiences. All the studies ensured that the perspectives of those involved were ethically included.

Practitioner research can be criticised because it may be seen as small-scale, anecdotal and non-replicable, or does not inform policy. I challenge this view because although there is much to learn from large national/international studies, I think that smaller-scale research helps deepen understanding and relevance at a local level. When teachers do this, it becomes context specific, offering them an opportunity to target their own practice, their own students' educational experiences, and inform school policy.

SENCOs are in a prime situation to collect evidence to support their work. They are immersed in the life of a school and have 'insider' knowledge and understanding that can enrich and aid investigations. Reviewing information from a range of perspectives and situations will strengthen evidence-based whole-school practice. Taking the time to do this is important, for as several of the SENCO authors in this book discovered, students' experiences can differ to staff perceptions, and both were needed to effectively meet the needs of young people with SEN.

The chapters

In Chapter 1, Tom Voice shares the experiences of new SENCOs in their first 100 days in post. He explores the key themes they identified, like dealing with the enormity of the new role, managing challenges with parents and developing new leadership skills. The chapter concludes with their advice for other new SENCOs, sharing what had been particularly helpful during their first term.

In Chapter 2, Jane Starbuck explores practical ways in which SENCOs can prepare for successful Ofsted inspections. She identifies what experienced SENCOs did to ensure that SEND provision in their school was robust and seen as everyone's responsibility, so that *all* leaders and staff were able to engage confidently with the process. The chapter concludes with advice from the SENCOs on what worked especially effectively during their inspections.

In Chapter 3, Emma Butler describes how her concern for young people to have a strong sense of 'belonging' in school led to developing new ways that increased their voice about matters that affected them. What started as an investigation into auditing the school's inclusive practice resulted in discovering some students who felt very vulnerable within school: something not previously known to staff. The chapter concludes with recommendations to consider interlinking issues of inclusion and empower students to become agents of change.

In **Chapter 4,** Emma Haywood shares how she embedded Makaton across the school to increase inclusive communication. She describes the activities that took place and how these impacted within classrooms and families, increasing confident interactions. The chapter concludes with recommendations about embedding and sustaining new practices, and the need to flexibly evolve such developments as new children join the community.

In **Chapter 5,** Eleanor Dorrington reports on how she led a development of teachers' practice of feedback through an evidence-based approach. She describes how this encouraged a collaborative way of working between teachers by sharing evidence of practice and enabled students to become active participants in the development rather than passive recipients of change. The chapter concludes with recommendations for leading school developments by building collaboration, trust and an environment where staff and student concerns are encouraged and managed with integrity.

In **Chapter 6,** Lauren Farrar describes how she introduced pre-teaching activities for maths with children who had found the subject very difficult and lacked the confidence to start learning activities without adult support. The activities' design was informed by children's feedback after discovering their negative experiences of previous interventions, and this new approach resulted in the children's increased enthusiasm and success in maths. The chapter concludes with recommendations for ways in which pre-teaching can be developed as a whole-school strategy to increase children's confidence and attainment.

In **Chapter 7,** Jemma Cotton explores the impact of limited wider-life experiences on pupils' social and academic inclusion in school. She describes how developing a programme of activities enhanced a group of pupils' social interaction, language development and academic progress. It also significantly increased their enjoyment of school, relationships with their peers and attendance. The chapter concludes with recommendations for using similar programmes to provide pupils with wider experiences so that they can engage more fully and confidently in school life.

In **Chapter 8,** Vanessa Mehta describes how she used an 'exclusion-proofing' strategy in school to investigate the barriers to attendance experienced by a group of boys. She collected their views through a 'word wall', interviews and a questionnaire, utilising these to provide individualised support and a wider whole-school programme. The chapter concludes with recommendations for how this strategy could be developed for overcoming barriers to inclusion experienced by other vulnerable groups in school.

In Chapter 9, Katie Hawksley explains how she developed a new whole-school referral form for staff to complete when seeking support for students with SEND. This required staff to provide details of what quality first teaching and other adjustments had already been trialled, with details of their impact, before additional support would be considered. While it took concerted effort to ensure that all staff consistently used this new process, the result was a referral system that was more streamlined, detailed and proactive, and did not rely on corridor conversations and ad hoc emails requesting support. The chapter concludes with suggestions for ways in which to design, and make accessible, a referral form to meet the needs of individual schools.

In Chapter 10, Michaela Brown describes how she investigated what all staff knew, understood and did, in relation to the school's SEND policy. A survey discovered inconsistent practice. Some staff's practice reflected what was set out in the policy but others did not, and some had not engaged with the policy at all. This led to further developments across the school that were successful in ensuring consistent practice for children. The chapter concludes with recommendations for auditing whether staff are following school processes and set practices, and following this with tailored CPD to meet particular group's needs, like midday supervisors.

References

Curran, H. and Boddison, A. (2021) It's the best job in the world, but one of the hardest, loneliest, most misunderstood in the school. *JORSEN:Journal of Research in Special Educational Needs,* 21(1): 39–48.

DfE (2022) *SEND Review: Right Support, Right Place, Right Time.* London: Department for Education.

DfE (2023) *Special Educational Needs and Disabilities (SEND) and Alternative Provision (AP) Improvement Plan: Right Support, Right Place, Right Time.* London: Department for Education.

Hattie, J. (2016) *Visible Learning into Action: International Case Studies of Impact.* Abingdon: Routledge.

Kay, V., Chrostowska, M., Henshall, A., Mcloughlin, A. and Hallett, F. (2022) Intrinsic and extrinsic tensions in the SENCO role: Navigating the maze of 'becoming'. *JORSEN: Journal of Research in Special Educational Needs,* 22(4): 343–351.

Chapter 1

SENCO's first 100 days

From feeling lost and exhausted, to growing in confidence and thriving

Tom Voice

> The last day of summer. Usually spent packing the school bag, re-stocking your shiny new pencil case, glancing at your time-table and thinking eagerly about your new classes. This was always the last day of summer as an English teacher. This year was different. I was returning as something else. Somebody else. I was returning as the SENCO!

The knowledge available for those interested in becoming a Special Educational Needs Co-ordinator (SENCO) in schools is frequently woeful. Schools' continual professional learning is often focused on developing pedagogy in the classroom in order to achieve progress. There is very limited understanding of pathways outside of the traditional progression routes within schools. Ask any SENCO whether they fully understood the role which they applied for and the answer will almost always be "no". Teachers need to hear from colleagues who hold the role of SENCO to understand the unique rewards and challenges which they will face. Only through hearing from colleagues who live and breathe the role day in and day out will they develop the knowledge to enable them to be confident and thrive.

Currently, over 1.5 million pupils in England have special educational needs and disabilities (SEND), an increase of 87,000 from 2022. During this time, the percentage of pupils with education, health and care plans (EHC plan) has increased to 4.3% from 4.0%, and those with SEN support but no EHC plan have increased to 13.0% from 12.6% (Gov.UK 2023). There has been a continuing trend of increases since 2016, with the proportion of children identified with SEND per class rising significantly, increasing demand for specialist support and funding; yet assessments for additional

DOI: 10.4324/9781003466550-2

funding may be refused or delayed. This creates a challenging context in which SENCOs must operate and navigate.

All schools must have a designated SENCO who is a qualified teacher working at the school, and this is the responsibility of the governing board. SENCOs are expected to oversee the strategic development of SEN policy and provision, ensuring the implementation of the school's SEN policy on a day-to-day basis. They are a key point of contact for colleagues, parents and students, offering support and advice for the identification of needs and suitable provision to meet those needs.

In reality, without significant support and mentorship, SENCOs can experience a wide range of challenges. The volume of tasks and range of responsibilities they are accountable for can become overwhelming. The national SENCO workforce survey (Boddison *et al.* 2020) stated that 30% of their respondents did not intend to still be in the SENCO role within the next five years, with nearly half (49%) citing workload as the primary reason and 70% feeling that they did not have enough time allocated to the role. This lack of longevity within the role is depriving students of experienced SENCOs who draw on a wealth of knowledge to overcome the constant and ever-changing challenges that the education system faces.

In order to support teachers who are often promoted to the role of SENCO with little experience of teaching or knowledge of how to support students with additional needs, SENCOs are required to complete a mandatory award. This is important to enable practitioners to develop a comprehensive understanding of the background legislation, policies and evidence that are key to inclusion and SEN provision. The award enables practitioners to secure their knowledge of inclusive practice and how to lead school provision.

New SENCOs' experiences

To discover the journey that SENCOs go on to move from 'surviving to thriving', a questionnaire was used to gain a range of views and experiences. Twelve SENCOs completed this from across a range of primary and secondary settings. The questionnaire contained three key focus areas:

1.   SENCOs' initial thoughts and feelings when appointed.
2.   SENCOs' reflections on their experiences at four different points in the first 100 days.

3. SENCOs' final reflection on the leadership journey they experienced during their first 100 days in post.

The key themes that were identified from their responses are discussed below.

Initial thoughts and feelings on appointment

Common themes from SENCOs' reflection about their feelings on the day before they started in their role were ones of excitement, trepidation and being grateful for being given the opportunity to undertake this unique leadership role. Some acknowledged that they felt they had limited knowledge in this area, making starting the role daunting.

Some had fears of fulfilling the role, related to their own level of SEND knowledge and potential challenges that might appear in managing members of staff, especially as the majority were stepping into their first leadership role. This uniquely challenging experience with SENCOs learning how to lead and to become an expert in a new area of school leadership was described by three SENCOs:

> Initially I was very excited about the role and this promotion was an achievement for me as I have wanted to move to the SENCO role for a number of years.
>
> (SENCO 3)

> I was terrified! How could I cover her [student] hours? How would I get her into lessons? The job hadn't even started yet and already I was getting sleepless nights.
>
> (SENCO 1)

> Initial thoughts/feelings, if I am honest, were that I actually had no idea what this role is and that having agreed to take it on I would be letting people down due to my lack of knowledge.
>
> (SENCO 6)

These viewpoints mirrored the emotions which I personally experienced upon being appointed to the role. I remember not fully understanding what the role would require due to it being a unique role which influenced all areas of school life. Another SENCO had similar emotions to me stating:

I was very excited and at the same time anxious about the school year to start. I was not sure at all what exactly I would be doing, reading the role description is usually not enough to have clear understanding of all the specifics and details related to the position in school.

(SENCO 7)

The first day

The SENCOs also described similar experiences at the end of their first school day in post, with a significant number talking of being 'surprised':

What have I let myself in for? There is so much to be done and so many children to get to know, I'm new to the school as well so I need to learn about the children but also about the school and the way things are done here.

(SENCO 10)

I felt innocent and stupid, even with the range of career experience I'd had, nothing prepared me for this job!

(SENCO 3)

I still feel rather shell shocked about having to do the role now!

(SENCO 10)

These voices are significant as they provide an insight into the fact that often new SENCOs have little knowledge of the breadth and depth of what is required by the role prior to appointment. This is because it is a role which staff frequently have very limited exposure to prior to being appointed, despite requiring SENCOs to become the expert in this area almost from day one. It could also suggest that the knowledge amongst other senior leaders within the school around the role of the SENCO and how to support their transition into the role could be limited. Often this role is line managed by an individual who has not held the role themselves and has limited knowledge of the complexity of what is required to be successful.

A few SENCOs spoke about the extremely beneficial support groups which they had found online or accessed via their multi academy trust. These supported them not to feel isolated in approaching this new leadership role – again possibly because this area of expertise is a skills deficit within other senior leaders.

The first week

When SENCOs were asked to reflect upon their first week, more common themes emerged. The central ones were the enormity of the job and the volume of workload. One SENCO described the first week as being "hectic, rushed, fast paced, ever changing, as I tried to clear my to-do list" (SENCO 12). It was clear that the majority of new SENCOs had devoted all of their time to the *operational* aspects of the role rather than undertaking any *strategic* considerations, which left them often feeling overwhelmed and deflated by the enormity of the role. Some described how, in order to manage the workload, they had to complete work in their own time to a greater extent than before. This increased level of personal commitment was described by one SENCO as feeling: "guilt towards my husband and son, as I was so shattered, they had to look after me" (SENCO 3).

SENCOs did begin to describe some of the early impact and success they were having in the role. Often this related to building positive relationships with parents, students or staff. One SENCO described the sense of success she felt by tidying her office and that this now gave her the headspace to approach the day in an organised manner. Clearly these small wins, which probably would not be noticed by anyone not in the role, represented an important step by which they were starting to take control over aspects of their day, as full control is something that can seem unachievable during this early stage of appointment. A further interesting comment from a SENCO described how they felt they were spoken to differently by staff members: the role had given them a whole-school profile and they felt providing advice to staff and supporting them meant they were, in return, treated with greater respect.

Half term

When SENCOs were asked to reflect on the main activities and issues they led during the first half term, they mainly described fulfilling statutory processes and completing operational paperwork requirements of the role. They appeared to have limited understanding of how these operational processes provided them with an opportunity for strategic leadership activities – for example:

- Challenges were approached on an individual basis, rather than using a surgery where pupils were discussed with external agencies to consider what recommendations could be used to influence whole-school practice.

- SENCOs described how they were frequently assigned the role of designated teacher for looked-after children and that this required them to attend multi-agency meetings. However, they made little comment on what leadership activities these generated.

A common theme running through the responses was that SEN-COs frequently felt they were the members of staff required to meet with angry parents who were unhappy with a school policy. This led to new SENCOs placing themselves under significant amounts of emotional pressure, which they described, using language like, "I survived to tell the tale". Often, they felt that they were managing complex parents' emotions, and parental expectations which were unrealistic due to the resources available.

The SENCOs who appeared to feel most successful in the role were those who had managed to lead on an identified strategy. One stated how she had successfully applied for the school to take part in a project across the local authority to support students' mental health needs:

> I was instrumental in raising the profile of Social Emotional Mental Health needs in the school. There was a big push on this area and I felt it was an imperative that we address it from a number of angles. I ensured that I had regular contact with our Young Minds Matter link worker in order to efficiently use the time which the school has been allocated.
>
> (SENCO 5)

Ownership over a project enabled SENCOs to see the difference that they can make to vulnerable students' lives, and this was instrumental in promoting a sense of success and commitment to the role. They could see that their efforts were worthwhile.

Another SENCO discussed how she was provided with a significant level of support from the Director of Inclusion. Whilst this was beneficial in providing support to manage her workload, she felt she was given little ownership over the tasks which she was completing and felt she had to ask permission to progress anything. The Director of Inclusion attended the Trust SENCO events, giving the perception that she was SENCO in name only and the power to make leadership decisions did not lie with her. This level of micro-management, while often well intentioned, needs to be carefully managed in order to ensure that a SENCO has the opportunity to develop fully in order to be successful in the role.

Professional learning during the first term had been rapid: most of the SENCOs discussed how the opportunity to engage with multi-agency teams was fundamental in developing their knowledge. They also spoke about how over the first half term they learnt the professional skills of time management, prioritisation and delegation. From my own experience of stepping into the role, learning how to effectively develop working relationships with a wide range of stakeholders was the most rapid learning point for me. The ability to chair meetings, hold external agencies to account and support parents to understand their role as co-educators was vital in allowing me to have impact within the role. These soft skills are probably the most significant ones for SENCOs to learn to achieve success.

The end of the first term and leadership

At the end of their 100 days in the role, SENCOs were asked to reflect on their thoughts and feelings about their first term. Across all responses it was clear that SENCOs felt they had developed their confidence and knowledge and had achieved success by staying in post and leading on the school's SEND agenda.

They spoke of looking forward to the holidays and how they hoped, with their newfound knowledge, that future terms would be less demanding. There was an acknowledgement that there was still much to learn and that they were hoping the statutory award would close the remaining knowledge gaps. A number also spoke about the personal accountability they felt for ensuring students with SEND were supported and they did at times worry that they had missed something. One SENCO stated that she hoped that "all individuals could see that the decisions she made were in the best interests of the children."

When asked what they would have done differently, a common theme was in relation to the leadership tasks they were required to undertake:

• They would have had more challenging conversations with staff members who they did not feel met their expectations.

- They would have taken time to map out the available external agencies to identify who to speak to and when. This would have saved them time in knowing who to approach when they needed additional advice or support.
- Prior to accepting the role, they would have requested more allocated time, enabling them to fully focus on the role.

When asked to reflect on what tasks they found the hardest, unsurprisingly the common themes related to the young people they supported. SENCOs described being required to talk to parents about their child potentially having SEND needs as being significantly emotionally taxing, with the conversation subsequently frequently revisited. One SENCO described how she was required to talk to a parent about a potential move away from mainstream school due to the behaviour challenges the child was experiencing. This was something which remained with them emotionally, as the parent was not supportive of the decision and a negative reaction was directed at them personally. This emotional response to managing the challenges that operating within the field of additional needs can create is something SENCOs have to learn to accommodate if they are to achieve longevity in the role.

One piece of advice for new SENCOs

Some of the most interesting responses from the questionnaires were in relation to the 'one piece of advice' which they would give to new SENCOs to help them in their first 100 days. Different themes emerged in relation to different aspects of the role. A common thread was the advice to take the time to get to know the students and parents. This suggests that considerable time is spent managing parental relationships and the tensions which often exist within these relationships.

Other comments related to self-care, with SENCOs advising future colleagues to pace themselves, not taking things personally. Their advice also related to accepting the variety of the role and that there will always be the need to ask for help. They recommended developing systems to support the management and organisation of job roles, and carrying a pen and pad to record odd jobs passed on to you, because things could get forgotten due to the huge volume of information which you are expected to absorb within the day.

Three SENCOs offered some final advice.

SENCO's first 100 days   21

Get systems in place that work for you so you don't miss things. Whether it is a physical note pad, a 'to do list' on Word, a white board pen etc. organisation is key! Also – always have a pad and pen on you as you will be stopped in the corridor on the way to the loo with a complex question!

(SENCO 8)

On the way home in the car I always spend at least five minutes reflecting on something positive – even if it was just a comment made by a student, or a mini conversation you had that solved a problem or changed someone's day. I'm learning that not everything a SENCO does can be measured by data.

(SENCO 1)

Never give up. You know more than you think you do. You are a champion for every child who is struggling in school. I know that teachers under the standards have overall responsibility for every child in their class, however, we as SENCOs have huge responsibility to help teachers see their potential.

(SENCO 2)

Recommendations

Recommendations for practice

- Identify the easy wins and act on one of them.

  The SENCOs who felt the most positive in the role were those who felt that they had an immediate impact on improving one aspect of the school's provision. This enabled them to gain satisfaction, seeing their considerable efforts were improving the lives of children. Examples of tasks that SENCOs completed included: designing a new SEND identification referral process; introducing a new SEMH intervention to address an emerging need; and holding parent workshops to improve parental communication and perception.

- Be organised.

  Map out the tasks which you will be required to complete over the first 100 days. This ensures that you can schedule time to be given to time-consuming tasks, like EHCP reviews or writing funding bids. SENCOs who did not take the time to consider which activities they would need to complete, and when, often described feeling overwhelmed and being required to commit a significant amount of their time outside of the school day to stay on top of workload demands.

- Create an organisational chart

  Create a chart showing the responsibilities, capabilities and interests of your team members. This will allow you to effectively delegate within your role. This ensures you know which tasks can be allocated to whom and who is likely to complete a task successfully.

Recommended reading

- Kay, V., Chrostowska, M., Henshall, A., Mcloughlin, A. and Hallett, F. (2022) Intrinsic and extrinsic tensions in the SENCO role: Navigating the maze of 'becoming'. *Journal of Research in Special Educational Needs*, 22(4): 343–351.
  The article uses four themes as lenses to explore how SENCO identities are formed and reformed by intrinsic and extrinsic motivators.

- Done, E. J., Murphy, M. and Bedford, C. (2016) Change management and the SENCO role: Developing key performance indicators of inclusivity. *Support for Learning*, 31(1): 13–26.
  This article provides interesting reading for SENCOs as it considers how SENCOs are now required to manage change strategically and deliver inclusive school cultures, rather than organisational activities.

References

Boddison, H., Curran, H. and Moloney, H. (2020) *National SENCO Workforce Survey 2020: Time to Review 2018–2020*. Tamworth: nasen.

Gov.UK (2023) *Special Educational Needs in England*. Available online at: https://explore-education-statistics.service.gov.uk/special-educational-needs-in-england (Accessed 07/02/2024).

Chapter 2

Preparing for Ofsted inspection

Don't prepare for inspection, do it because it is the right thing to do

Jane Starbuck

For most SENCOs the term 'Ofsted' creates sleepless nights. However, when the new Education Inspection Framework (EIF) was introduced in 2019, I was excited. No longer, it seemed, could schools achieve a good or outstanding grade for quality of education if provision for special educational needs and disabilities (SEND) was poor. This means that conversations about SEND would not just be the domain of SENCOs. They would now be a whole-school responsibility, with all staff needing to discuss SEND and how they could collaborate to adapt provision for students on the SEND Register. For many SENCOs this has been a real challenge. How can they ensure that the whole school is prepared to meet the needs of students with SEND and also demonstrate that everyone can confidently articulate this to an Ofsted team?

We asked this question in a survey for SENCOs to determine how they managed the Ofsted experience. Their responses highlighted how they rose to the challenge. There were several similar themes, but perhaps the most important message was to prepare your school to *understand* SEND and not just to be *prepared* for Ofsted – SENCOs should work with staff to enable them to be more confident with the Ofsted process so that they can 'shine'.

> Don't prepare for an inspection by preparing for an inspection.
> Do the right things for your kids and it will shine through.
>
> (SENCO 1)

What is the right way to prepare for discussions with Ofsted about SEND? It is important that this is viewed as a whole-school priority and not just the function of SENCOs. It is about ensuring there are robust whole-school systems in place so that everybody – leaders,

DOI: 10.4324/9781003466550-3

governors, curriculum leads, teachers, teaching assistants, and young people and their families – is confident in their understanding of how the school makes provision for young people with SEND.

So, what is it that SENCOs need to actually do to make sure that SEND provision in their school is robust and is seen as everyone's responsibility to ensure that, when Ofsted arrive, *all* leaders and staff can engage with confidence?

Preparing all staff to ensure that SEND is everyone's responsibility

Leaders

SENCOs emphasised the need to meet regularly with leaders so that developing provision is seen as a collaborative process and everyone is confident talking about SEND. One SENCO highlighted the need for:

> Coaching for staff on how to articulate provision to the Ofsted Inspector.
>
> (SENCO 9)

If a SENCO is facilitating support using a coaching approach, what do they need to make sure leaders are confident about?

- Leaders must be knowledgeable about their statutory responsibilities towards children with SEND, with a good understanding about the content of Chapter 6 of the Code of Practice (2015), which is currently 19 pages long. This informs schools about the need to use 'best endeavours' to support children with SEND, along with the requirement to appoint a qualified teacher as SENCO, who must achieve the mandatory award. There is an expectation that leaders understand the four broad areas of need and how the school's graduated approach meets these needs.
- SENCOs need to work closely with leaders to ensure everyone understands the 'Vision' for SEND in their school, that there is a shared understanding of what this means, and how it impacts everyday practice. Are all staff able to articulate the vision and explain how it is reflected in policy and practice? Do school leaders understand that every teacher is responsible for the progress and provision for their students with SEND?

- The School Inspection Handbook OFSTED (2024) staff how their school can evidence the quality of provision to meet SEND needs. The statements in the EIF regarding SEND should be shared to ensure all staff are aware of Ofsted's requirements and can identify how their school is fulfilling them. One SENCO in our survey posed these questions to staff and asked them to work together to evidence what the school was doing to meet needs. This created a shared understanding and built confidence.

> We prepared answers for questions that were likely to be asked by Ofsted – this was VERY useful as they did ask several questions which we had prepared for.
>
> (SENCO 5)

The role of a SENCO should be that of a SEND *Coordinator* and *Leader*, not the 'SEND *Do*', or creator of all SEND provision. As SENCO 7 points out, this can be difficult if they are not on SLT or don't have a very clearly defined route into SLT to ensure their voice is heard:

> The team needs to be joined in cohesion with each other. If a SENCO is not on the leadership team or a DSL, you can have problems with relaying information, however, you make it work and ask the DSL if there is anything that you need to know.
>
> (SENCO 7)

Curriculum/middle leaders

The importance of ensuring all leaders, including middle leaders, are confident in meeting the needs of students with SEND was emphasised by our SENCOs. Middle leaders play an important role in the Ofsted process, so it is important they have support.

> I met with curriculum teams and prepared aide memoire A3 sheets to 'script' responses – kept everyone on 'the same page'.
>
> (SENCO 3)

> We do something called 'challenge partners' once a year and involving our middle leaders was really key to us being able to talk about our work and knowing what to expect, similar to

an interview – the practise of talking about our school really helped.

(SENCO 8)

To guarantee that SEND is everyone's responsibility, it is important for SENCOs to work in collaboration with middle leaders, as they are responsible for monitoring the quality of teaching in their subject area to meet the needs of all learners: they need to be able to track progress for the SEND cohort and be clear about which students are making progress. If a student is underachieving, they can work with the SENCO to identify what support is required to meet need and enhance progress. When curriculum leads monitor their subject, they need to identify how barriers to learning are removed for individual students with SEND. SENCOs can support curriculum leads to understand how the curriculum can be adapted for the broad areas of need and how the recommendations from 'SEND in Mainstream' (EEF 2020) can be developed to create adaptations for their subject area.

Teachers' responsibility

The Code of Practice (2015) is clear that teachers are responsible and accountable for the progress of students in their class. When a student fails to make progress, it is then the responsibility of the teacher, working with the SENCO, to assess whether the student has SEND.

All the SENCOs we questioned stressed the importance of developing teacher confidence and skills to meet the needs of young people with SEND. Ultimately, *every* teacher is a teacher of SEND. As a SENCO it is important to remove the misconceptions that only specialists can teach students with SEND or that the SENCO is responsible for making provision for those students. They should ensure that all teachers are aware of their own responsibility, as illustrated in Teacher Standard 5 – 'Adapt Teaching to respond to the strengths and needs of all pupils'.

One SENCO highlighted that at their school SEND was always a focus when engaging with teachers, so it was recognised as part of their teaching role:

Ensure EVERYONE was on the same page! It was very clear that through each classroom visit/deep dive/staff interview,

SEND was a focus. It was not a separate entity, and we were praised for the consistency across school.

(SENCO 5)

SENCOs should work closely with teaching and learning leads in schools to ensure that time is allocated to develop a shared understanding of what adaptive practices are and how they can be used to support all children, particularly those with SEND. Some SENCOs produced adaptive-teaching posters as a reminder for staff. Time is needed to focus on particular strategies to ensure there is a consistent understanding, with confidence in how they are used and what impact they make. In one inspection, a SENCO was asked to describe what adaptations teachers made in specific lessons and their impact.

Class teachers are expected to map the interventions received by the children in their class and to implement the CPD offered, with specific focus on meeting needs of SEND learners through reasonable adjustments.

(SENCO 4)

Developing the school as a learning environment is a key consideration. SENCOs can develop staff understanding about the importance of the school environment. Too much clutter can create sensory overload. Do students know how to use the information on working walls, is key vocabulary clearly displayed? Leaders can influence the type of environment students work in and ensure staff consider what it feels like to work in their rooms. Staff should consider seating positions, access to labelled equipment and sensory overload. Discussions about consistent environments can be useful. Consider, for example, will we all have and use a visual timetable, will key words be displayed in certain areas?

The graduated approach

We had a meeting to ensure staff knew the key points they needed to be doing as class teachers. I provided a graduated approach flow chart to refresh memories and went through what we need to be doing for children with SEND/concerns.

(SENCO 2)

This SENCO prepared a flowchart to ensure that staff understood the Graduated Approach in their school and the processes that supported it. On receiving the 'OFSTED call' they checked in to ensure that all staff remembered this process. It is vital that all staff understand the 'Assess, Plan, Do, Review' process and their role in it. Successful SENCOs have clear expectations about what they expect to see before a staff member raises concerns that a child may have SEND, like evidence of trialling a range of adaptations and strategies designed to meet the child's needs.

Many SENCOs have introduced referral forms for raising concerns to ensure there is a consistent approach. It is only after observing a cycle or two of this support and monitoring the impact that a SENCO can decide if further assessment is required and a student needs to be placed on the SEND Register. There should be clarity about assessments available to monitor the progress of a child's needs in all of the four broad areas. One inspector particularly liked an "Inclusion flowchart which maps out what we do and which aspects are for 'keeping up' and which are for 'catching up' " (SENCO 1).

Be a strategic SENCO

What does this mean in practice and how does that support the school in being prepared for Ofsted?

A strategic SENCO will have a development plan that focuses on improving provision for SEND. This understanding of priorities will ensure that the SENCO is aware of any required CPD and will be able to build this into the whole-school calendar. SENCOs should not provide all the CPD, but can signpost or link colleagues with particular areas of strength.

> During the meeting the inspector asked if I had the NASENCO qualification and when I had completed it. He wanted me to talk about 'What SEND looked like in the setting' – specifically what he would see whilst touring the school.
>
> (SENCO 6)

Strategic SENCOs will know what SEND provision looks like throughout the school and how individual staff adapt their practice to support it. They need to observe practice in classes and ensure that CPD has had an impact on classroom delivery. SENCOs need a planned timetable of activity for each term, with dates booked in to ensure specific activities are actioned. This can include EHCP reviews, CPD and monitoring.

SENCOs spend significant time producing and sharing information with staff, so it is vital they monitor that this information is used effectively to meet the needs of pupils with SEND and can further inform the development plan. Monitoring of provision is something that can be missed due to time pressure, but it is vital to ensure strengths and areas for development in school are identified. This forms part of the 'OFSTED Conversation' and as SENCO 3 explains, in-depth knowledge of provision enables this to be showcased to Ofsted:

> Try to shine. Know what you do well and make sure that message gets through. Tell colleagues so that you sound like a broken record.
>
> (SENCO 3)

Involve families and students

Inspectors often cross-checked information provided by staff with the students. When asked if they would do anything differently to prepare, some SENCOs talked about how involvement of families and students was an area for improvement.

> We had a questionnaire for parents and children on the SEN register to ask their views on what we could do better and what they wanted to hear.
>
> (SENCO 7)

Involving families and students throughout the whole SEND process means that a SENCO has a full understanding of the parent and student voice. Involving them in developing pupil passports, and reviewing the impact of support, ensures their voices are represented. The SEN Information Report, published on the school website, provides evidence of support available in school. SENCOs could create a working group to further develop this, so that parents and carers can ensure it is written in a language that is accessible to them and reflects their experiences.

Keeping information up to date and shared

In preparing for Ofsted, a number of SENCOs stressed the importance of keeping their own records up to date. This meant regularly reviewing the SEND Register and ensuring that information regarding students' needs, assessment data and the impact of interventions was built into their calendar of activities. It is critical that staff know how to easily find the information pertaining to SEND so they can quickly access it for use during inspection.

> I ensured paperwork was maintained (education plans, up-to-date B Squared assessments, evidence of personalised learning by ensuring pupil files were up to date) to inform case studies and discussions.
>
> (SENCO 4)

Ofsted inspectors often want to see how EHCPs inform provision for students. SENCOs might need to summarise the content of an EHCP so that staff can translate this into practical targets and strategies within learning plans. Ultimately, the SENCO's main role should be quality assurance, to ensure that targets are appropriate and that strategies and actions planned are relevant. Ofsted may use these plans to evidence that an EHCP is reflected in classroom practice:

> He tracked three students' provisions from EHCP to IEP to planning, teaching, marking work and setting appropriate next steps. Then corroborating with a student voice exercise. He was very much interested in how we followed through processes.
>
> (SENCO 3)

What did the inspectors ask you?

The SENCO survey consistently identified two questions that were asked.

What is the school's vision for SEND?

A shared vision is vital. This clearly articulated vision should be reflected in all policies and practices throughout school. SENCOs must "Ensure everyone is on the same page".

How do teachers and TAs provide support?

To be able to support TAs and teachers, SENCOs emphasised the need to understand what is considered 'best practice'. They then worked with leaders to identify ways this could be adapted to fit the context of their own school. If teachers are to retain responsibility for pupils' learning and assessment, how are teachers and TAs able to plan intervention and support? TA contracts do not always enable opportunities for face-to-face meetings, so schools need to identify how they can use the systems they have to support this.

As a SENCO it is vital to know and understand the strengths and development needs of their TA team. A skills audit is a useful tool to identify what training, experience and interests the team have, and their potential CPD needs. This also helps when considering succession, so that if a team member leaves, leaders know what gaps need to be filled. Creating an induction process for staff is good practice. This ensures staff feel supported when they join the team, but also creates a consistent level of understanding around expectations for SEND. Often when there is training on teaching and learning TAs are not invited, but they need to have a good understanding to be able to transfer this knowledge to support the pupils they work with. Some may have particular specialisms, so it is empowering to encourage them to share this knowledge/expertise with all staff. Schools need to be learning environments for everyone.

'Making Best Use of Teaching Assistants' (EEF 2021) has developed a number of useful resources (like the 'Scaffolding Framework' and 'Teacher TA Agreement') to support schools in developing the way teachers and TAs work together. It is important that teachers also understand these messages so that practice is consistent and thoroughly understood.

What evidence did you provide that Ofsted inspectors particularly liked?

The survey identified a number of practices that SENCOs felt Ofsted considered to be real positives in their schools.

a) To be able to speak confidently and provide evidence of adaptations that schools used was viewed by this SENCO's inspector as a particular strength:

> The adaptations in the classroom – books for children with dyslexia, special board for writing, staff leading a small

group (4 children) who had manipulatives to support their learning and how staff involved the children to be independent, digital support with individual IPads; the enhanced provision mirroring a special school practice.

(SENCO 9)

b) 'SEND in a Nutshell'

A number of SENCOs commented that being able to provide a 'SEND in A Nutshell', or a '1 Page Profile' was liked by inspectors because this tool provided a simple, but clear, summary of the school's SEND profile. It evidenced an ability to articulate what SEND looked like at an individual school level and understanding of how to develop practice based on the needs of the school. It could also be shared with all stakeholders to inform and act as a platform to discuss SEND within school.

c) Files

Other SENCOs gained confidence in developing a file which contained examples and elements of their work that reflected how their school developed policies and practice to meet the needs of the students with SEND.

I prepared a file which 'showcased' the policies, procedures and documentation linked to the provision in school, such as SEND Action Plan, Policy and Information Report, Pupil Passports, Provision and Intervention maps etc.

(SENCO 4)

d) Case studies

The use of case studies to showcase how school had developed provision to meet the needs of particular students was identified as a positive activity to evidence the impact of support on young people, and reminded staff how the right type of support could make a difference to students' lives:

I prepared case studies to evidence progress of individuals and to show how the provision has been tailored and adjusted to meet individualised need.

(SENCO 4)

What *one* piece of advice would you give to other SENCOs about OFSTED inspections?

> Know your children in and out, and what provision you have in place for them.
>
> (SENCO 7)

This message was abundantly clear in SENCOs' responses – make sure you know your students on the SEND Register well. Understand their special educational needs, their barriers to learning and also their strengths – what is the child good at and what are the things that interest them? This knowledge is key for staff to understand when developing any support and building a positive relationship.

Children learn when they feel safe and secure. They need to have a trusting relationship with staff so that they feel safe to take risks and adopt new skills. Children need to feel that they belong in a school and in their class. Ultimately it is the teacher who can create this sense of belonging. If they do not feel this, they will struggle to learn and make progress.

> The most important thing for me was not to apologise for my high expectations to staff, not to allow short cuts and slipping in day-to-day provision; keep explaining and insisting on full inclusion.
>
> (SENCO 9)

SENCOs also emphasised the importance of knowing the staff team well so that it was possible to highlight their strengths to inspectors.

> Just making sure you knew your team, so you could talk about their strengths.
>
> (SENCO 8)

One SENCO felt that demonstrating the impact of support was important and had produced documentation that evidenced this. Knowing what, and how, provision is making a difference to young people on the SEND Register is crucial.

I RAG rated IEP targets so that we had a one-page document highlighting the progress of children against their targets. This was vital as we were asked how we assessed progress.

(SENCO 5)

SENCOs clearly identified that the key to preparing for Ofsted was to develop a whole-school understanding of the SEND needs of children, along with systems and practice that met these.

Know all of your children with SEND and what you do for every single one of them. If you don't know, find out. If there's nothing to find out, sort their provision out. If you don't like what you've found, sort their provision out. Then the day will be easy.

(SENCO 9)

During conversations with inspectors, SENCOs found it useful to have documents to hand to act as evidence to support discussions – it was important to be able to access them quickly.

Make sure you know where to find information/documents. Have them to hand, as a few times I was talking about an area, and I was able to show him what I was talking about, which helped.

(SENCO 2)

A strong leader knows their school, and this applies equally to SENCOs. They need to be able to talk with confidence about the strengths of SEND provision, but also able to identify the next development areas. They should be able to celebrate what is working well but not be afraid to articulate reasoning behind plans for the future.

Be honest about what is working well and areas of improvement, they will triangulate everything that you say.

(SENCO 6)

Finally, the most important piece of advice came from SENCO 4, who was clear that while SENCOs have a vital role in school, SEND is the responsibility of every governor, leader, teacher and staff member who must ensure that their everyday practice creates an environment and provision where all students can thrive:

> The one piece of advice I would give is, do not wait until you are due to have an OFSTED inspection to ensure you are prepared, you should be prepared anyway because you should be ensuring your policy, procedures and provision are in place regardless, and if you do not feel prepared, seek support and guidance because you do a really important job . . . and you don't do it for OFSTED.

(SENCO 4)

References

Department for Education and Department of Health and Social Care (2015) *Special Educational Needs and Disability: Code of Practice: 0–25 Years*. Available online at: https://www.gov.uk (Accessed 22/03/2024).

Education Endowment Foundation (2020) *Special Educational Needs in Mainstream Schools*. Available online at: www.educationendownment foundation.org.uk (Accessed 22/03/2024).

Education Endowment Foundation (2021) *Making Best Use of Teaching Assistants Guidance Report*. Available online at: TA_Guidance_Report_ MakingBestUseOfTeachingAssistants-Printable_2021-11-02-162019_ wsqd.pdf(d2tic4wvo1iusb.cloudfront.net) (Accessed 22/03/2024).

OFSTED (2024) School Inspection Handbook. Available on line at https:// www.gov.uk/government/publications/school-inspection-handbook-eif/ school-inspection-handbook-for-september-2023#evaluating-behaviour- and-attitude.

Chapter 3

Capturing voices. Increasing all students' experience of belonging in school

Emma Butler

Context

I work in a mainstream secondary school in the Midlands, where 8% of our community are of Eastern European background and 47% of employed people work in low-skilled, low-paid jobs. Our cohort are predominantly white and approximately 30% qualify for Pupil Premium. We have 36 children with EHCPs (education, health and care plans) in our school (three of which are in our post-16 provision) and we also have a small specialist setting attached to our school which has an additional 20 students with EHCPs.

Have you ever not had a voice? It is a very disconcerting position to be in. As a white, middle-class person, this was something I was completely unfamiliar with until I joined a particular Facebook group. It changed my perspective completely.

I became aware of an online community in which autistic and ADHD adults give advice to other adults who are, in some way, responsible for the caregiving to autistic and ADHD young people. The group's aim is to improve the experience of today's young people and educate others into practices and perspectives which can be harmful to someone who is neurodivergent.

The rules of the group clearly state that you are not allowed to comment unless you are neurodivergent yourself. The group is quite vocal on how harmful a neurotypical person can be when they have opinions on the support of neurodivergent children, but have no personal lived experience. In this group, therefore, I do not have a voice.

In the beginning, this was a novelty. I was able to read the posts and subsequent comments in an attempt to educate myself in how I could best support my students and my autistic foster daughter. I learnt a lot about ABA (applied behavioural analysis) and was

DOI: 10.4324/9781003466550-4

able to reflect on my own practice in school. However, at times, the lack of voice was stifling and oppressive. Someone asked about the EHCP (education, health and care plan) process in the UK – I was unable to answer. Sometimes, a post would make me feel real concern about the young person at the centre of it and the apparent attitudes of the adults around them. Again, I was not allowed to comment. My voice is something I had always taken for granted. Belonging to this group led me to two conclusions:

1. Many people, and a high number of young people (whether they have additional needs or not) do not have a voice. As adults, we are very good at using our perspective to inform decisions. Aren't we the experts, after all? The voice of the young person is often disbelieved or not taken seriously – this experience awakened in me that having a voice is fundamental to my existence and should therefore also be fundamental to the existence of the young people I have the privilege to support.

2. Cemented by the course of study for my NASENCO award at Nottingham University was: 'Nothing about us without us.' This was a key theme which we revisited time and time again. I now have less certainty in my own voice – not because I am not experienced, but because I have not authentically lived the experience of someone who is neurodivergent or has another type of additional need. For a while, this led to a crisis in confidence and the feeling that I had lost my credibility. However, over time and by continually educating myself, I know I do have a powerful role to play within inclusion. My role now centres on collecting the voices of others and educating myself to become an advocate for the young people I work with.

Developing whole-school practice

When completing my research, I had only worked in this school for a few months. I knew that we needed to move towards a more inclusive model but was unsure where to start. Given my interest in 'voice', I decided that I needed to truly understand the voices of those around me, before determining a strategic plan to implement. I could see areas which needed work, but the most important part of my role would be to take the team with me – I needed to identify how I could find and communicate a 'why' that would resonate with them.

When considering 'voice', it is also essential to consider other voices in the school community: those of the staff would be particularly pertinent to developing my understanding of the current position of the school. One area which had fascinated me was that of our 'own lens', which was going to be an even more important consideration when trying to capture the true voice of colleagues.

We come to all situations with assumptions and preconceived beliefs – our 'lens'. In order to truly understand the voice of someone else, we have to consciously strip this back, which is incredibly hard to do. Removing our own lens is not completely possible. But what is possible is being acutely aware of our own lens, recognising how it changes our interpretation which therefore enables us to take this into consideration. I had decided that my initial information gathering needed to be via an extended narrative interview. This would then allow me to formulate a strategy for completing the main body of my research project.

Collecting evidence to measure impact

Evidence collection

I created three research questions to ensure my focus was tight and clear:

1. What is inclusive practice?
2. What is the understanding of the difference between integration and inclusion?
3. Which external factors (race, gender, social class, sexuality, labels such as SEN, 'low ability' or EAL) contribute to practice not being inclusive?

My position as an 'insider-researcher' was crucial. My findings needed to lead to positive change, not the alienation of some staff. The data I collected must be used in an honest, but sensitive, way. I also had to consider my role in school and how teachers may respond to questions – I needed to reassure all volunteers that this was a research project driven by a desire to understand the school's position (rather than the position of one individual) in order to implement positive change. That discussion took place prior to interviews. This was important, given my role as a new leader in the school. The entire focus of the project was to ultimately lead to an enhanced experience for ALL students in school and so I needed to secure the faith and commitment from the teaching staff.

I used four modes of collecting evidence:

1. An initial teacher interview
2. Seven subsequent teacher interviews
3. A questionnaire to all teaching staff
4. Four student focus groups (students with English as an additional language, students who identify as LGBTQ+, students with additional needs, students who qualify for Pupil Premium)

Permission was sought by the head teacher to complete my research project. The teachers who were interviewed were all volunteers – this was also the case for those who completed the survey. In order to gather the voice of the students, permission was sought by the young person and their parent/carer. The teacher interviews were held on Teams and were recorded so that the voice was recorded accurately. This meant there were opportunities to revisit the interviews and improve my understanding of what had been said.

The initial interview had a broad focus – it was designed to help inform which questions would then be posed to subsequent teachers. The responses were also used to pursue avenues of information gathering. All seven subsequent teachers were asked the same questions:

1. Can you please tell me how you ensure that your practice is inclusive and which groups of students do you believe have barriers to inclusive education?
2. And generally, as a school, how inclusive do you think we are? What do you think we do to cater for the needs of all children?
3. And what about the wider school community? If you think about after school clubs, the Junior Leadership Team, stuff like that – how do we include all students in that?

The questionnaire (see Figure 3.1) was responded to by 23 out of a possible 70 teachers. Although this was a low number and could reflect a lack of interest, it is important to contextualise this response. None of the seven teachers interviewed responded to the questionnaire – they could have believed they had already contributed to the project. The questionnaire was circulated towards the end of the summer term. The academic year had been extremely challenging and leaders had less disposable time than normal. These factors could have negatively impacted the response rate.

Teachers' Questionnaire

Name:

1. Define 'inclusive practice in education'

2. What is the difference between integration and inclusion?

3. How inclusive do you think we are as a school?

1	2	3	4	5	6	7	8	9	10

Not at all inclusive   Extremely inclusive

4. Rate the following in terms of their importance as a barrier to inclusion in education:

	Not at all important	Slightly important	Fairly important	Important	Extremely important
Being identified as 'PP' or 'FSM'					
Being identified as a student for whom English is an additional language					
Being identified as having an additional need					
Being part of the LGBTQ+ community					
Being identified as an ethnicity other than White British					

5. What would enable you to develop your understanding of inclusive practice? Tick all that apply:
    ❑ Coaching following lesson dips
    ❑ Specific understanding of diagnoses
    ❑ Support to implement Quality First Teaching
    ❑ Further Student Spotlight sessions
    ❑ Understanding the experiences of students
    ❑ Training to understand, interpret and support behavior
    ❑ Training to understand the key elements of inclusive practice
    ❑ 1:1 support from Emma Butler
    ❑ Other ....

Figure 3.1 Teachers' questionnaire.

The student focus groups were arguably the most interesting part of the research. There were eight students present each time with a notetaker so that we could accurately capture what was said. We all sat in a circle together and I had prepared questions to pose (the same for each group). If a student made a point which I felt warranted further exploration, I was responsive to this and the discussion followed this thread. This was important as I wanted to really understand what was being said and only posing strict predetermined questions would have inhibited this process. The questions were as follows:

1. What do you understand about the term inclusive education?
2. Can you think of any reason why some students might not feel included in school?
3. Let's start to think about the 'school' rather than the students. Do you think all opportunities are on offer to all the students at 'X'?
4. Have you always felt included in break and lunchtime?

Impact

Staff

The initial interview was very long – it was time consuming to transcribe and there was lots of information to navigate. If I were to complete another project, I would have put a time limit on responses to make contributions more focused.

The examples of inclusive education given by teachers were dominated by one common theme: know your students. This was reassuring and demonstrated that teachers were interested in the individual. Although these responses were encouraging, there was some deficit thinking which impacted the detail of their responses. It was universally agreed that more needed to be done to encourage all to have an active role in the wider school community and some positive ideas provided about how to increase engagement.

Some responses revealed a variety of normative beliefs held by colleagues, such as these two regarding students who qualify for FSM:

> They haven't had the books, the colouring, all the stuff that our children have probably had.

> Because they come from a poor background, their parents aren't so motivated, they find it quite hard, they have not seen anyone progress, so they don't take education very seriously.

Uncovering some of the beliefs of colleagues was uncomfortable at times. It was surprising that these beliefs were held about students from families with lower incomes – were teachers lowering their expectations and aspirations for these students? These assumptions did not necessarily reflect a lack of drive to support students, but it became apparent it would be essential to remove deficit thinking to ensure that some children do not underachieve because they are perceived as destined to do this.

The interviews also revealed some positive understanding of how to support students with perceived barriers:

> I know what makes me a good teacher, compared to possibly others, and it's going to sound really big headed, it's about establishing relationships with them.

> I very much teach to the individual.

> So, I think first you need to know your children.

One element of the project was to understand what was being done well in the school, in terms of inclusive practice. It was evident we had a core group of teachers with an appetite to teach to the individual. Promoting and spreading this culture would form part of the next steps for our academy. An individual approach was a relief to hear:

> We don't call it an overlay, we call it the Window to the World, she quite likes calling it that instead. Or just the blue window. It's more discreet, she prefers it to be called that.

The questionnaires provided a variety of definitions for 'inclusive education'. The most successful provided details regarding which groups of students needed to be considered when defining this term – all respondents included students with additional needs. Only one respondent included multiple groups of students, including those with EAL and those who qualified for pupil premium funding. Given that I was the school SENCO at the time, this tied into the lens through which teachers were framing their answers.

This always needs to be considered so that, when interpreting data, context and external influences can be taken into account.

It was interesting that some perspectives varied significantly between teachers and students. One example of this was for the group of students for whom English is an additional language. Teachers responded with:

> I honestly just don't know where to begin with an EAL student.

> We are good at identifying them, but I'm not convinced we have done enough, as quickly as we could, to accommodate them in the classroom.

However, students responded:

> It does not matter where you are from and what you look, like they just think about education and teachers and students are very helpful.

This highlighted some potential anxiety regarding how to cater for these students, but their lived experience did not reflect this. They acknowledged that it was hard to be in English-speaking classrooms but accepted this was natural and understandable and felt appreciative of the support they received. This linked with outcomes for students with EAL – who outperformed the whole-school cohort last year in terms of their outcomes and Progress 8.

Students

All the students were really happy to contribute – this was very reassuring and made for lively and animated discussions. Interestingly, the students seemed to not be as impacted by external factors compared to the teachers. They relaxed into the conversations very quickly and it did not feel as if this was a discussion with a 'teacher'. Overwhelmingly, students reported that all opportunities were available to everyone in school. This clearly demonstrated a position of inclusion. All groups stated that social times were the most difficult in school and sadly provided clear examples of feeling excluded from the school community – students were able to report lived experiences, even if they were someone else's. It was clear this would need to be an area of focus for the school to improve.

The group who identified as LGBTQ+ perhaps provided the most shocking responses. However, their experiences weren't reflective of their opinion of 'the school':

> The school does not care who we are, as long as we are good students.

The barriers to inclusion, identified by the whole group, were their peers. This was not expected:

> People spit and kick.

> People tell you to go kill yourself and tell you that you disappoint your family.

> I was holding hands with the same gender – I was told to slit my wrists.

It became apparent that these experiences were happening daily and students felt it was driven by a perceived 'difference' to the 'norm':

> There is a culture of being unkind and when they find out that you are different, they use it against you.

It was interesting to note that this 'group' was not once raised in a teacher interview and the overwhelming majority of questionnaire respondents did not see this characteristic as either extremely important or important. These experiences were hidden or not being recognised in school. One student commented about a teacher's response:

> Yes, the teacher did nothing, just told us to stop talking. I told her it was making me feel uncomfortable and she listened to what he said and just blanked him.

This lack of direct action clearly led to the student feeling vulnerable and unimportant. Addressing this would be vital for the school to move forward on the continuum of inclusion – **all students must feel safe in school.**

It was most challenging to gain the views of the young people with additional needs – their learning and communication needs meant that their voice needed to be heard in a way that validated their opinions, not in the detailed way I perhaps wanted it to be articulated. Responses were brief but valid and it was important to not distort their voice to satisfy the need for detail.

It became clear, through all the data collected, that normative beliefs were a barrier to inclusion; the experience an adult brings to a setting forms their own belief system and assumptions – these can be difficult to challenge. However, conversations around these are essential. As educators, we should all believe that learning is life-long. Challenging assumptions does not mean confrontation is inevitable – two-way dialogue is a powerful tool.

It also became apparent that, as a school, we were not maximising the use of one of our most powerful agents of change: the students themselves. We needed to consider how to amend our power relations and start to empower the young people we are there to serve – the opinions gathered were insightful, real and impactful.

Recommendations

Recommendations for practice

The exploration of 'voice' and 'lens' genuinely impacts my practice every day. My interactions with students, colleagues, parents and other professionals now have a different level of understanding – I try to listen to really understand, rather than listen to reply (something most of us do, most of the time).

I have also used my research experience to further explore and understand the experiences of students within the whole school community. For example:

- When 'Everyone's Invited' became prevalent in the UK media, there was a sharp focus on the need to understand how young people experience incidents regarding consent and sexuality.
- Having discovered through my initial research project that there was a persistent and negative experience for students who identified as part of the LGBTQ+ community, we then held female focus groups and LGBTQ+ focus groups in each year group. The results were startling and shocking – they identified patterns and behaviours which were seriously impacting the experience of some children in school. We were then able to take a range of actions to mitigate the risks and communicate this work openly in the school community.

Uncovering concerns of this nature can be disconcerting, but it is so important to pursue a valid voice and then tackle difficulties which may be happening in school. **Be brave but be ready: if you ask the questions, you will get the answers.**

Recommendations for leading whole-school development

It was important to first reflect on what I had learnt holistically. It is impossible to understand what needs to change without actively listening to the reason a school exists: the students. Gathering their perspective has demonstrated that students need to not only be subject to change but *agents of change*. This requires an ethos of respect – where power relations are acknowledged and dissected.

Normative beliefs are a barrier to inclusion. It can be difficult to challenge the experience an adult brings to a setting formed from their own belief system and assumptions. However, conversations around these are essential. As educators, we should all believe that learning is life-long – and as a leader, I aim to use my new knowledge to influence others. Challenging assumptions does not mean confrontation is inevitable – two-way dialogue is a powerful tool for leaders.

Recommendations

- Communicate the 'why' more effectively. My vision is for our school to embrace all students – it is not only a vision for students with additional needs
- Share the voice of students – encourage colleagues to take this information and use it as a springboard for improving their own practice. Use this knowledge to discuss inclusion and develop a vision of what that means for all stakeholders
- Build an understanding of 'Inclusion' to embrace all 'differences' and recognise the negative impact of labels
- Secure an understanding of the difference between integration and inclusion in order to empower practice through knowledge
- Challenge, by raising awareness, that dominant discourses disrupt the core values of inclusive practice. Work with the member of SLT responsible for outcomes of students from low-income backgrounds

- Conduct coaching lesson dips to establish how QFT is currently used
- Work with the leader for students with EAL needs to promote confidence and identify broad/individual training needs
- Work with a bespoke SEMH support tool, such as 'Thrive', to focus on improving and supporting the well-being and resilience of all students
- Work with the whole school to promote a culture of being kind

Recommended reading

- Bishop, R., Berryman, M., Cavanagh, T. and Teddy, L. (2009) Te Kotahitang a: Addressing educational disparities facing Maori students in New Zealand. *Teaching and Teacher Education*, 25: 734–742.

This piece is particularly interesting to explore the inherent assumptions which can be made regarding 'groups' of people and the way this can impact expectations and aspirations.

- Gillborn, D. (2010) The white working class, racism and respectability: Victims, degenerates and interest-convergence. *British Journal of Educational Studies*, 58(1): 3–25.

This piece again discusses assumptions made – this time it focusses on assumptions made about families and backgrounds. It was particularly interesting to hear the opinions of educators and about how their beliefs were impacting on their classroom practice.

- Nilhom, C. and Alm, B. (2007) An inclusive classroom? A case study of inclusiveness, teacher strategies and children's experiences. In Soler, J., Waksh, C. S., Craft, A., Rix, J. and Simmons, K. (Eds.), *Transforming Practice: Critical Issues in Equity, Diversity and Education* (pp. 103–114). Stoke-on-Trent: Trentham Books.

This piece helped to highlight and demonstrate the concept of inclusivity being a journey, rather than a destination. It was very reassuring to understand that small steps are, in fact, the only way to move along the inclusivity continuum.

Chapter 4

The magic of Makaton interaction throughout the school

Emma Haywood

Context

Situated in a small ex-mining town, my nursery school has been 'Outstanding' for over 20 years. There are 101 children enrolled, offering 15- or 30-hour places, with each morning or afternoon session having up to 65 child places available. The staffing structure consists of myself, the head teacher, as well as two teachers, one higher level teaching assistant, eight nursery nurses (working part and full time), two care assistants and three office workers. The school is predominantly composed of White British working-class families (96%), and has pockets of high-level deprivation, with 22 of our families receiving Early Years Pupil Premium (additional funding for early years providers to help them improve education for disadvantaged three- and four-year-olds). Speech and language is a focus for the school, with 28 children either receiving support from a Speech and Language Therapist or ECAT (Every Child a Talker) intervention within school. Our school is signposted by professionals for families with children with special needs, so we currently have nine children with EHCPs (education and health care plans), who receive a high level of funding.

I believe communication is key to inclusion, and from observing closely the interactions of specific children with high levels of special educational needs (SEN) within my setting I felt that although their key workers communicated effectively, there was a clear barrier for the children to understand and communicate with staff and peers. My school needed to be a more cohesive community, one which encouraged and celebrated all achievements, not only within school but in the wider municipal. In Shah's book, a disabled learner called Mike points out explicitly how inclusion is important

DOI: 10.4324/9781003466550-5

when he explains, 'I'd make it easier for any disabled person not to feel as left out and excluded, because we're not freaks or anything, we're just the same (as non-disabled people) except they haven't got as much limitations' (Shah 2009: 102).

This understanding that all children need to feel they are part of a community is essential, and communication is fundamental. Having observed a selection of children with SEN within school and already seen first-hand the need to improve the communicative environment for these individuals, I felt that my initial reflections for the need to change was complete; now I needed to focus on the research.

Developing whole-school practice

School leaders have a major role to play in developing and improving this learning environment for others. This wider school climate influences all staff, and if the head teacher is a 'lead learner' he or she has to demonstrate in practice their own orientation towards learning.

(Crawford 2014: 40)

As a head teacher, I lead on 'learning' in all forms. New initiatives need to derive from firstly the need for change and then what research is already available to show that a new initiative will provide the desired impact.

The EEF (Education Endowment Fund) website clarified my thinking that the first stage for ensuring a quality education for children with SEN is to 'Create a positive and supportive environment for all pupils, without exception' (EEF 2020), but unfortunately, I did not find enough specific information on 'how' I could achieve this and so I met with my speech and language therapist. We discussed what would make the most impact on not only individuals but the whole school in terms of communication and creating opportunities to improve friendship, and social skills. The use of Makaton as a whole school began to take shape, and so I now had a focus for my research.

Firstly, I needed to find out about what Makaton was and how it had been introduced within schools. I began to read about children with SEN and what impact Makaton signing within their environment had on their sense of inclusion.

One text called *Working With Hannah* supported my thinking. Here, Glass and Wise (2000) delve into the life of Hannah, a child with Down syndrome, and her journey through a mainstream infant school. The book highlights Hannah's initial struggles in developing friendships, as well as aspects of personal and physical care. More importantly, it highlights how introducing Makaton at a whole-school level was critical and how guaranteeing the right level of support can make inclusion a success, for not only the children and family but also for the school itself.

Senior Leader Kris Campbell Cauldwell introduced Makaton at a whole-school level and argued that 'Embedding Makaton into school life helps to ensure every child and young person is supported to express themselves and understand their environment' (Campbell Caldwell 2023).

Reading these first-hand accounts on the impact of introducing Makaton clearly resonated, as this was the long-term vision for my school!

I began by introducing the project to my governing body through injecting this into the School Improvement Plan, because I knew that to embed successful change, it had to become part of our whole-school vision. My next step was ensuring that my staff bought into the project, for, as Cowne et al. state, 'Understanding the principles behind the change management process helps individuals and organisations to transition more effectively' (2015: 104).

During a staff meeting I gave specific examples of when staff had struggled to understand what a child was trying to communicate, as well as examples of lost opportunities for peer-to-peer exchanges within play. We had open discussions on what the team felt were the barriers to these connections and the staff were open about their differing levels of understanding around Makaton. It was important that my research was emancipatory in principle – that is, carried out *with* staff and not done *to* them – so it was important to include their thoughts. I understood through these discussions that over the years some team members had been Makaton trained, but now felt de-skilled, and were openly reflective on how they had stopped using Makaton within school. Some team members had never heard of Makaton. I explained that to begin my project I needed to have a firm understanding of their individual level of Makaton competency and so all staff highlighted the Makaton signs they knew on a vocabulary list from the Makaton website (www.makaton.org). This became my baseline audit.

I had already identified three children within my setting who were chosen due to their specific communication and language challenges. All three children used either some Makaton or non-verbal actions to communicate and so, I felt, they would benefit from a positive impact on peer-to-peer communication. This project was aimed to have an impact on the incidental interactions between peers and staff, so a baseline was needed to ensure the most accurate correlation at the end of project. I decided to use two short ten-minute observations, one at the start and another at the end of the project. To enable me to accurately compare the observation data, I devised a sheet that converted interactions into data by using a tally of specific types of exchanges:

- Adult to Child: Verbal Only
- Adult to Child: Makaton and Verbal
- Child to Adult: Non-Verbal (i.e. point, gesture)
- Child to Adult: Makaton
- Peer to Child: Verbal Only
- Peer to Child: Makaton and Verbal
- Child to Peer: Non-Verbal (i.e. point, gesture)
- Child to Peer: Makaton

Now I had a firm baseline of staff knowledge as well as observation data, I liaised again with my speech and language therapist to facilitate a starter Makaton training session with the whole staff team to build confidence so that change can take place. The 1.5-hour interactive training involved understanding the impact of introducing Makaton, learning and practicing key signs and symbols. Following the initial training I arranged a senior management team meeting to discuss how, as a school, we could begin to implement Makaton into our everyday practice alongside supporting families to ensure the project had a legacy.

It was decided that weekly Makaton signs would originate from the 'book of the week' and be integrated into planning – for example, when this was 'The Three Little Pigs', the weekly sign was 'pig' and families were encouraged to use the sign when reading the story. Specific signs that directly impacted on the daily life of children with SEN such as 'more' and 'help' were to be taught explicitly. Makaton signing was to be used on the gate when greeting families, and the teachers, HLTA, nursery nurses and care assistants were to model using Makaton during continuous play opportunities, and specifically in daily story and snack/lunch sessions. We wished to encapsulate Kris Campbell Caldwell's point that 'Ensuring everyone uses signs and symbols everywhere, all the time, means every pupil is respected and included in all areas of school life' (2023).

This also included working with parents. During the Makaton baseline audit, it became clear that one member of our team was very proficient at Makaton, so I approached her to use this skill to support another nursery nurse, and together I wanted them to oversee Makaton within the online learning provision. Together the two nursery nurses provided families with a weekly Makaton sign, story and rhyme.

These strategies aimed to follow Bonner's practice (2023) which found that training and supporting parents deepened the impact of Makaton interventions, because children who were supported consistently both at home and in nursery developed their verbal and nonverbal communication at a faster rate.

Collecting evidence to measure impact

Evidence collection

Three months later it was time to review the impact of all activities within this research project. This review took the form of finding the impact from the viewpoint of staff, parents/carers and children. For the adults within this project, information was gathered from two questionnaires, as well as asking the staff to complete a further Makaton audit to look for progress in knowledge. I constructed these questionnaires by creating questions that provided predominantly statistical data responses, while the final question was strategically left open ended to allow personal reflections on the project. This enabled respondents to comment on topics they might not have previously considered.

The final undertaking was to look at the impact on the three children who were originally observed. I carried out the exact same observations, keeping time scales and recording sheets the same to ensure fair comparisons wherever possible.

Impact

Staff audit and questionnaire

Tables 4.1 and 4.2 show the numbers of staff (14) that undertook the Makaton audit at the beginning and end of the project. With the exception of two members of the team, there was a good response

Table 4.1 Staff knowledge of Makaton signs at baseline and end of project

Role	Response	Number of Makaton Signs Known	
		Baseline	End
Teacher	Y	56	90
Teacher	Y	73	160
HLTA	Y	130	156
Nursery Nurse	Y	58	87
Nursery Nurse	Y	52	94
Nursery Nurse	Y	154	160
Nursery Nurse	Y	83	136
Nursery Nurse	Y	24	97
Nursery Nurse	Y	167	215
Nursery Nurse	Y	25	84
Nursery Nurse	–	–	–
Care Worker	Y	16	46
Care Worker	Y	5	22
Office Staff	Y	12	49
Office Staff	Y	3	3
Office Staff	–	–	–

Table 4.2 Staff average increase of Makaton signs known

Type of Role	Number of Staff Submitting a Response	Average Number of Makaton Signs Known		Average Increase
		Baseline	End	
Teacher	2/2	65	125	+60
HLTA	1/1	130	156	+26
Nursery Nurse	7/8	80	125	+45
Care Worker	2/2	11	34	+23
Office Staff	2/3	8	26	+18

to the request. Table 4.2 shows that there was an increase in Makaton knowledge across all sections of the staff, especially for the two teachers who had an average increase in 60 signs known. The results suggest that office staff improved their knowledge, but with an increase of 18, this was not at the same rate of other roles.

Table 4.3 indicates that at the end of the project, half of staff are using Makaton in at least 75% of their sessions, compared to only two using Makaton on this scale at the beginning, which points to an overall increase in the amount of Makaton signing used by staff within teaching sessions. Staff who answered 1–3 for Question 4 were asked to give reasons behind the low percentage. Office staff were more isolated from the children and so as one member of staff understandably explained, their lack of Makaton was "due to the nature of our work, the office has limited contact with staff and children". A few members of staff indicated further training would help, as well as "repetitive use and practice". Others suggested raising the profile again so that staff are "just being more aware to do it", with a suggestion of "Maybe we could have a board in the staff [room], with several signs on it, to try and use for that week".

The results shown in Table 4.3 suggest that Makaton signing was mainly evident with child-to-adult interactions compared to peer-to-peer. When asked if Makaton was more evident in nursery, 14 members of staff clearly indicated 'Yes', with two saying they didn't know. These two staff members were office staff.

Staff were asked to add further comments to show the impact of the project. These were in some cases reflective in nature, as one staff member stated, "On a personal note I need to use Makaton more". Overall staff commented that the method of the project had been positive:

> Staff have been supported to develop their levels of confidence to deliver their practices and to support our children and also to support our parents in their ability to use signing to support their children at home too.

> We have some outstanding staff in School who use Makaton naturally and proficiently.

Parent/carer questionnaire

A questionnaire was sent to 101 families about their experience of the Makaton online learning and 31 parents/carers responded. The results indicated that all of the parents/carers who took part in the questionnaire were aware of the Makaton online learning posts and had also shared at least one of the activities with their child. Results

Table 4.3 Staff use of Makaton signs in their work

	Never	25% of my sessions	50% of my sessions	75% of my sessions	100% of my sessions
Q1. Before the Makaton training how often did you use Makaton within your teaching/work sessions?	3	6	3	2	0
Q2. How often do you currently use Makaton within your teaching/work sessions?	1	2	4	5	2
Q3. On a scale of 1–5, with 1 being 'never' and 5 being 'frequently', how often do you see children using Makaton with adults?	0	7	4	2	1
Q4. On a scale of 1–5, with 1 being 'never' and 5 being 'frequently', how often do you see children using Makaton when communicating with their peers?	5	6	3	0	0

also indicated that 28 of the children had used a Makaton gesture outside of school with seven children using Makaton with another child. This suggests that Makaton interventions were leading to children using Makaton in a more natural way in an unstructured environment.

Through the use of a final open question, the parents/carers were able to give their reflections on the project. One parent/carer stated: 'My child really enjoys learning and using Makaton, even though it's not her main form of communication' and another highlighted: 'It's great that G comes home and teaches us all signs. I fully support this and should be practised in all schools and colleges'.

Observations of the three children

Table 4.4 shows the total number of interactions for all three children during the baseline and end of the project observations. The results from just these two ten-minute monitoring activities show a notable increase in the amount of Makaton used by adults with the children and the start of peer-to-peer Makaton interactions.

Summary

This research project originated through an identified need to improve peer interactions for children with special educational needs. The aim of the project was to utilise teaching opportunities within a nursery setting to not only teach the staff, children and their families some Makaton signs, but to provide opportunities and confidence to use Makaton to support communication.

Table 4.4 Comparison of interactions used by adults and peers with the children

Type of Interaction	Baseline	End of Project
Adult to Child: Verbal Only	26	9
Adult to Child: Makaton and Verbal	3	15
Child to Adult: Nonverbal i.e. Point, Gesture	7	3
Child to Adult: Makaton	2	12
Peer to Child: Verbal Only	33	23
Peer to Child: Makaton and Verbal	0	4
Child to Peer: Nonverbal i.e. Point, Gesture	8	5
Child to Peer: Makaton	3	8

The results from the staff training indicate that staff are now more equipped to use Makaton within our nursery, with the exception of the office staff who have not had the opportunity to use and refine their Makaton knowledge over time. On the whole, staff are using Makaton more frequently in teaching sessions and the staff, who on reflection did not use the communication method as frequently as they could, were able to provide suggestions to improve their overall performance i.e. "Maybe we use some of their [Makaton-confident staff] skills to support less confident users". One member of staff summed up the impact of their journey with the statement:

> Any learning journey needs a balance between having the space to respond personally, and also the opportunity to work collaboratively for support and impetus. The project has allowed people to work at their own pace, it has made space for people to use Makaton in the context of planning and it has also encouraged people to use and role model it with children in real time, e.g. snack.

It is therefore recommended that Makaton training not only needs to be a whole-school approach, but also needs to be regularly reviewed to ensure consistent success.

The impact of staff knowledge and application is translated into the results from the Parent/Carer Questionnaire that indicates that children were using Makaton signing outside school and some of these were used during interactions with peers. However, it must be noted that only 31 out of 101 families asked to complete the questionnaire participated and so this data is not fully secure.

The online learning opportunities had enabled parents/carers to carry out Makaton activities with their child leading to a better understanding of the nonverbal communication, as these comments suggest:

> Lots of parents are commenting that they are using Makaton at home, teaching them and their siblings too. Parents are encouraging them to sign 'Good Morning' on the gate, and lots of them do now.
>
> (Staff)

> [It is] Important for all children to learn Makaton so non-verbal children can also interact with friends.
>
> (Parent/Carer)

The observations carried out on the three identified children with SEN indicated that Makaton was starting to become part of the natural communication between adults and children and more importantly between children. These observations show the clear positive impact of using Makaton within home and school teaching opportunities on peer-to-peer interactions for children with SEN.

Overall, the results show that this project is starting to have a direct impact on the interaction of children with SEN at my school and ultimately as Cowne et al. state:

> For embedded change to succeed, it has to become a whole-school vision' and this project not only needs to become part of the school's ethos, but it also needs to continually evolve to ensure continued success year on year with new cohorts of children.
>
> (2015: 103)

Recommendations

Recommendations for practice

- Clearly define your problem or barrier to learning for individuals or groups of children.
- Carry out research – this includes talking to professionals within your community.
- Consider 'what has gone before'. This will enable you as a leader to consider how you are going to deliver this to staff. If an initiative has been carried out before, you may have resistance and so you must plan for this.
- When introducing your project/initiative provide examples of why you wish to make a change. Make these clear alongside your aim for improving the opportunities for the individual or group of children.
- Consider ethos and culture. Involve others in your planning so they feel part of the process and look for opportunities to grow individual staff to lead and mentor others.
- Think about how this new practice will be sustained and embedded.

Recommendations for leading whole-school development

As a leader, this project emphasised to me the importance of building a culture for change. In order for change to happen and have lasting impact, your staff team needs to be empowered, knowledgeable and skilled to implement your desired project.

At the end of my project the results showed that there were some staff who still used Makaton in less than 50% of their teaching sessions. On reflection, regular bite-size staff training would keep the momentum and would constantly build on staff knowledge. This, alongside facilitating mentoring from more confident staff, would support individuals identified as needing additional support.

Following this project, I implemented many suggestions made by the staff within the final questionnaire, including displaying the focus signs around nursery. The use of Makaton within my school continues to evolve, but it now has a firm foundation in supporting our most vulnerable learners.

Recommended reading

1. Putting Evidence to Work – A School's Guide to Implementation (EEF). Available online at: www.educationendowmentfoundation.org.uk.
The Education Endowment Foundation is a website dedicated to research and is funded by the Department for Education. This guide supports strategic leadership in providing a step by step approach to implementation.

2. Your Stories. Available online at: www.makaton.org.
The Makaton Charity website is a good starting point to find out about Makaton and the site has a number of case studies of how Makaton has been incorporated into schools and early years settings across the country.

References

Bonner, L. (2023) *Essential Early Years*. Available online at: https://makaton.org/TMC/News_Stories/Your_stories/At_school/EssentialEarlyYears (Accessed 20/02/2024).

Campbell Caldwell, K. (2023) *Willowbank School*. Available online at: https://makaton.org/TMC/News_Stories/Your_stories/At_school/WillowbankSchool (Accessed 20/02/2024).

Crawford, M. (2014) *Developing as an Educational Leader and Manager.* London: Sage Publications Ltd.

Crowne, E., Frankel, C. and Gerschel, L. (2015) *The SENCO Handbook: Leading and Managing a Whole School Approach.* Abingdon: Routledge.

Education Endowment Fund (2020) *SEND Evidence Review.* Available online at: https://educationendowmentfoundation.org.uk/ (Accessed 20/02/2024).

Glass, C. and Wise, L. (2000) *Working with Hannah: A Special Girl in a Mainstream School.* London: Routledge.

Shah, S. (2009) *Young Disabled People: Aspiration, Choice and Constraints.* London: Routledge.

Chapter 5

Developing classroom practice through evidence-based leadership to increase the achievements of pupils with SEND

Eleanor Dorrington

Context

My school, based in an East Midlands city, is part of a multi-academy trust and is an average-size primary school with 328 on roll. The percentage of pupils with identified special educational needs and disabilities (SEND) is 14%, which is just above national average for academies. The school also has 77% of pupils from minority ethnic backgrounds and pupils who speak English as an additional language (EAL) is 55%, over double the national average. Most of these children arrive at the school with little or no English and this was their first admission to a school in this country, or in any school. The most recent census also recorded that 43 different first languages were spoken.

At the start of an academic year, I introduced a new way to assess pupils with SEND who were working well below age-related expectations (ARE), to track their small-steps progress. Both myself and teaching staff felt the label of 'well below' was not only negative, but it also prevented us from identifying any progress the children were making. From using this new form of assessment it became clear when analysing the data in upper key stage two (UKS2 – Years 5 and 6) that those working well below ARE were making fewer small-steps progress in maths, compared with reading and writing. In the spring term, UKS2 pupils with SEND made an average of three small-steps progress in maths, compared to six steps in reading and five steps in writing. This highlighted a key area for development for the UKS2 staff and therefore became the focus of my research project.

DOI: 10.4324/9781003466550-6

Developing whole-school practice

I decided that in my development as a leader in the role of SEND Coordinator (SENDCo), it was essential for me to use this opportunity to improve my skills in leading others to bring about change and improve outcomes for pupils with SEND. As Cowne et al. (2018) explain, SENCos are 'change agents' and must support staff in meeting the needs of pupils as well as enabling them to meet the demands of everyday teaching. Beaton et al. (2021) also argue that the moral purpose of leadership – primarily the intention of making a positive change – is at the core of being an effective school leader. In my role as SENDCo, this is what I aim to base all of my decisions upon. I feel that leading inclusion is leading change and therefore, for me to make a positive impact on outcomes for pupils with SEND, it was key for me to start by identifying what changes needed to be made.

It has been consistently shown that high-quality, effective and accessible feedback is integral to effective teaching and has a direct impact on academic performance, particularly pupils with SEND (Newman *et al.* 2021; EEF 2019; McLeskey *et al.* 2017), so this is essential in every classroom. For my research project, I decided to support teachers in UKS2 to implement a new approach to providing feedback to pupils with SEND in their maths lessons. This would enable me to implement the principles of effective leadership whilst simultaneously enabling UKS2 staff to pilot a new initiative before I introduced this as a way of whole-school working. As Cowne et al. (2018) explain, trialling change with a small group first enables leaders to practice and develop their skills as a leader of change and become a better, more effective leader in the process. For the purpose of this study, the nine pupils with SEND from UKS2 were participants along with their five class teachers.

To implement the new approach, I first presented the relevant research to the five members of UKS2 teaching staff in a team meeting. In this session, I also gave them a summary document to support their continuous professional development (CPD) and ensure they understood why I had chosen to pilot this in their classes. It was important for me as a leader to provide opportunities for staff to understand the motivations and evidence, as well as the process of change. This approach of evidence-based leadership has been widely discussed as being a high-efficacy approach that enables all stakeholders to have clarity and a shared understanding of what is being done and why (Cowne et al. 2018).

Following the meeting, I provided training to the staff, explaining the new approach to feedback, discussing the elements of high-quality feedback and demonstrating how it could be implemented using an online teaching platform. This gave myself and the staff time to discuss the benefits of the approach as well as any difficulties they might face. Once staff had begun using the new approach on a daily basis, I met 1:1 with each teacher to: i) discuss the progress of the pupils and how the project was going and ii) to share ideas to make the process easier and ensure pupils with SEND were making progress as a result of the feedback given. This reinforced the collaboration between all stakeholders to create a trusting, transparent environment (Jones 2018).

Collecting evidence to measure impact

Evidence collection

To enable me to track and maintain control of the process of change, I chose to use an action-research approach, which involved the cyclical process of planning for change, implementing actions, analysing the outcome and reflecting upon these in order to develop next steps. The approach allowed for a collaborative experience with other staff members, which additionally supported my leadership development.

I also identified that a child-centred approach would enable the children's voices to be heard and guide the project. This was something which I felt was important because I believe 'pupil voice' is key in all aspects of educational leadership, and as a result, the pupils were active participants within the research rather than being 'passive' recipients of change. By using this approach, I was able to collect a variety of data from different sources and include a range of perspectives for my findings.

I used four main data collection methods: semi-structured and structured interviews, questionnaires and progress data.

Before staff implemented the new approach, they were given two questionnaires: the first regarding feedback in their general classroom practice and the second specifically focussing on maths. These questionnaires were given out to complete at the beginning of a staff meeting. I felt allocating a specific time for this was important so that they were able to focus fully on their answers. The questionnaires asked staff to detail key aspects of feedback for pupils with SEND, such as the barriers they face as staff when giving these pupils feedback on their learning in maths, how effective they felt the current methods for providing feedback were and whether the feedback for pupils with SEND differed to those without SEND.

Pupils were also asked several questions in structured interviews. These interviews were conducted by myself: however, I only felt comfortable doing this as all the children knew me well and had been taught by me previously. This is another aspect I felt was important, as I wanted the children to feel calm and confident. They all took place in a quiet learning space that the children were all familiar with, again to try and put them at ease. During these interviews the children were asked how their teacher gives them feedback, what feedback they are given, how this helps them in their learning and what they liked about the feedback. This enabled me to gather the children's perspectives and shaped the way I instructed staff when using the new approach.

After the approach had been trialled for eight weeks, staff then took part in semi-structured interviews. I felt the semi-structed approach would be useful as it would enable staff to explain in more depth their views on the new approach whilst also giving areas of focus to allow for comparisons between staff and their classrooms. In these interviews the following questions were asked:

1. How effective do you think the new approach to feedback is? Why?
2. What was the impact of changing the approach to feedback in maths?
3. What challenges or difficulties did you face when implementing the new approach?
4. How do you think this approach will support pupils with SEND in other subject areas?
5. How were you supported in embedding this new approach in your classroom practice?
6. What would help you to continue implementing this method and/or make further changes to the way you deliver feedback in the future?

The children were asked the same questions again in structured interviews and data was collected in regards to their progress scores. By using the various different methods I was able to gain different perspectives whilst exploring the impact upon current practice and progress of pupils.

Impact

Comparison of the two structured interviews (pre and post new approach) with the nine pupils showed that they were all able to articulate how feedback helped them following the change. Most explained in the post-interview how the new approach to feedback helped them improve in their learning. For example, Child 6 said that: "It helps me because then I can try the harder challenges" whilst Child 2 stated that the feedback helps, "So I know what I got wrong so I don't get it wrong next time and can get better at maths." Similarly, Child 5 stated, "It helps me know how to do the questions." This showed that the new approach was having a positive effect on both the children's academic progress and their view of themselves as learners.

Following the introduction of the new approach to feedback, the nine pupils with SEND in UKS2 all made more small-steps progress in the term after the new approach was introduced compared to the term before. As shown in Table 1, all pupils made at least four more small steps of progress other than Child 2 who made one additional small step of progress compared to the previous term. Despite the one child making only slightly more progress, the data indicates that the new approach overall had a positive impact on the children's progress in maths.

The semi-structured interviews with teachers following the introduction of the new approach identified its impact. It also highlighted the key skills of effective leadership that I had begun to develop, as well as raising areas for me to improve further in my role as a leader of change. Every teacher commented on the positive impact that the new approach had upon their pupils with SEND. For example:

> It was something the children engaged really well with. It is most effective for children who struggle to read or struggle to focus when I am giving whole class feedback.
>
> (Teacher A)

> I'm so pleased to see the difference it has made to the children. It means they are able to access the information more easily.
>
> (Teacher C)

Teachers were also asked to give feedback on my role in leading the project and what impact this had on their practice. They commented on the usefulness of having had regular meetings, as well as initial training. Teacher B for instance answered:

> I found it useful to look at the examples, as it was a bit daunting at first.

Whilst Teacher E said:

> We had meetings throughout where we could talk about our problems . . . so this made it easier for me to put it in place more regularly.

From analysing the teachers' feedback, **three** themes emerged. Firstly, it became evident that building and fostering trust was one of the most important factors in my role as a leader of change. Three out of the five teachers commented on feeling confident and motivated to be part of the change process as a result of the safe environment they were in, where mistakes could be made and any problems shared with the team – for example:

> Although the approach was tricky to use at first, I found that the supportive ethos we have within our team enabled me to discuss with you and others what the difficulties were and we solved the problems together. I think I would have found the process much more difficult if I didn't have this support.
>
> (Teacher A)

> Because we had everything explained to us really clearly and you were very honest that you were not expecting us to know all the answers straight away and that this was a trial to see what the impact would be, it made me feel much more confident and I knew I could come and ask you for help if I needed it.
>
> (Teacher C)

The second theme was the impact of using evidence to explain *why* the approach had been chosen. Most of the teachers reported that the training session, where the reasoning was shared with staff, was very useful. They also explained how having access to the journals, books and other evidence that I had based my research upon made it easier for them to understand what was being done and why:

I think we are often told to introduce new ways of doing this, that don't make sense or we don't understand the reasoning behind it. As we had all the information presented to us and we discussed it in detail, it felt like we were part of the process and involved more in the decision of how to make the change. I think because we were all invested in this it meant we were more motivated and excited to start the project with you.

(Teacher E)

The training was very interesting and I liked having the journals and books to look at that talked about the theory behind the approach. I also found it useful to look at the examples.

(Teacher B)

The third theme was the importance of clear, consistent communication and the opportunity to communicate with myself as the leader at different points throughout the process. All the teachers commented on the value of having the opportunity for open learning conversations and how this helped them throughout the project. Teacher A explained that:

I really liked being able to talk through any problems I was having. We also had time in our team meeting on Mondays to chat with the other teachers to see how they were getting on and shared ideas of how to make the process quicker.

Similarly, Teachers C and D described:

We regularly met as a team once we had started and we discussed any issues we were having. This gave us a chance to feed back to each other as well as to you so that we could continually try to make changes and improvements to the way we were implementing the approach to make it the best fit for the children in our classes.

We had lots of support throughout the process of trialling this new method of feedback . . . and several meetings throughout the term to catch up on what extra support we needed.

Another important finding from the interviews with staff and children, as well as anecdotal evidence from the regular meetings with teachers, showed the impact of using pupil voice. As part of the initial interviews with pupils I explained that we wanted to know their views throughout the project and requested that staff have regular check-ins with each pupil to see how they felt about using the new system. I believe this made the pupils feel involved from the start and that they were valued as part of the process. During one of our weekly meetings, Teacher C shared how, as a result of their check-in discussions, two of the children in their class had requested to use headphones to access the feedback online. They discussed how the pupils reported they really enjoyed this – they felt it removed distractions and made them less self-conscious about listening to feedback in front of their peers. This led to all pupils in the project using headphones when accessing their feedback as other staff members felt this may be beneficial to trial with pupils in their classes too. In subsequent team meetings, staff reported that this was having a positive impact on pupils' engagement with the new online system for providing feedback. This was also evident in the follow-up interviews with many of the children, like these two, explaining:

> I can use the headphones to listen to the video . . . I can play it lots of times if I get confused.
>
> (Child 4)

> I like listening to the videos on my own on the Chromebook so I know how to get better and make less mistakes.
>
> (Child 8)

This impact was highly useful for demonstrating to staff why we should always consider involving the children and getting their feedback on such processes. In this project the views of pupils enabled staff to create changes and therefore help make our new system more effective.

Recommendations

Recommendations for practice

The new approach was shown to be highly effective and directly impacted upon progress scores in maths for children with SEND. I believe this was due to staff providing highly personalised feedback in an accessible way for their pupils. As the approach allowed them to record feedback through various different modes (e.g. audio recording, drawing, video etc.), this also reduced workload, thus making staff want to use this approach more widely. I would therefore recommend that staff consider the modality of feedback, not just for pupils with SEND but all pupils as this can directly impact how effective their feedback is and thus impact upon progress.

This process also highlighted the importance of including the children when introducing a new approach to any classroom to ensure it accurately meets their needs. Their feedback on the process was just as useful as that from staff as they were able to precisely communicate what they felt about the new approach rather than an adult trying to interpret their preferences. This enabled me to support staff in making the approach to feedback more suitable for the pupils and therefore making the approach more effective. This also reinforced the notion of 'nothing about us without us' which I feel should underpin all decision-making in relation to SEND practices.

Recommendations for leading whole-school development

After completing my research project and reflecting upon the process I would highly recommend ensuring any new approaches or changes are implemented in a collaborative manner. Both myself and the members of staff involved felt that the new approach to feedback was more effective because they were made to feel part of the process and were therefore more invested.

I also feel creating a trusting and honest ethos was very important for me as a leader and is something all leaders should aspire to do. It is clear from the literature that successful strategies for implementing change are often underpinned by the environment and those environments which have high trust and honesty enable leaders to establish integrity and create 'buy in' to any changes. I strongly believe that as leaders we must provide a forum in which others can express concerns as well as discuss any opposing views. Through the regular 1:1 and team meetings, I could see the benefit of this aspect of leadership as it not only supported the staff, making them more confident and motivated, but also allowed me to practice my skills as a problem solver.

Another recommendation I would suggest when implementing change in schools would be to ensure you, as leader, are continuously reflecting upon your own leadership throughout the process. As a result of my critical reflections during this research project, my leadership style began to change. I was able to see what aspects of my leadership were more effective in supporting both staff and children and where improvements could be made. As school leaders we are often very busy and therefore may not prioritise activities such as reflection, however as a result of this project I can see how useful it can be and this has impacted upon how I will approach implementing change in the future.

Recommended reading

1. Bush, T. (2020) *Principles of Educational Leadership & Management*, 5th ed. London: Sage Publications Ltd.

This book is very useful for new and experienced leaders as it provides an explanation of theories and approaches to leadership in schools that are up-to-date as well as discussing ways in which these can be implemented in every day practice.

2. Teacher Feedback to Improve Pupil Learning – Senior Leader Implementation Pack by Education Endowment Foundation (2021) Available online at: https://educationendowmentfoundation.org.uk.

This is a document that can be used by school leaders to develop effective feedback policies and approaches in their schools, and provide a clear, simple summary that can be shared with teaching staff.

3. Beaton, M. C., Codina, G. N. and Wharton, J. C. (2021) *Leading on Inclusion – the Role of the SENCO*. Abingdon: Routledge.

This book is highly useful for SENCos as it examines the leadership of SEND specifically, discussing tools and strategies that support effective SENCo practice.

References

Beaton, M., Codina, G. and Wharton, J. (2021) *Leading on Inclusion: The Role of the SENCO*. Abingdon: Routledge.

Cowne, E., Frankl, C. and Gerschel, L. (2018) *The SENCO Handbook: Leading and Managing a Whole School Approach*, 7th ed. London: Routledge.

Education Endowment Foundation (2019) *Improving Teacher and Pupil Feedback – EEF Scales Up Embedding Formative Assessment Programme*. Available online at: https://educationendowmentfoundation.org.uk/news/eef-scales-up-feedback-programme (Accessed 27/02/2024).

Jones, G. (2018) *Evidence-Based School Leadership and Management: A Practical Guide*. London: Sage Publications Ltd.

McLeskey, J., Barringer, M.-D., Billingsley, B., Brownell, M., Jackson, D., Kennedy, M. and Ziegler, D. (2017) *High-Leverage Practices in Special Education*. Arlington, VA: Council for Exceptional Children & CEE-DAR Center.

Newman, M., Kwan, I., Schucan-Bird, K. and Hoo, H.-T. (2021) *The Impact of Feedback on Student Attainment: A Systematic Review*. Available online at: https://d2tic4wvo1iusb.cloudfront.net/documents/guidance/Systematic-Review-of-Feedback-EPPI-2021.pdf (Accessed 27/02/2024).

Chapter 6

Making a difference with successful pre-teaching

Lauren Farrar

Context

The primary school I work in has 312 pupils, 34 of whom are eligible for free school meals. There are a small number of children on the school roll who are from minority ethnic backgrounds: none of these children are at the early stage of learning English. Most of the children at the school are White British. The proportion of disabled pupils and those who have special educational needs supported through school action is above the national average, with 49 on the 'watchful eye' register and 32 on the special educational needs (SEN) register. Two pupils are supported with an education and health care plan (EHCP). The majority of children on the SEN register have cognition and learning as their main area of need. Our school SEND policy states: 'As a school we provide a safe, stimulating and inclusive learning environment' and appropriate provisions are in place that ensure all pupils can overcome barriers to learning so they can fully access the national curriculum.

Developing whole-school practice

After taking over the Special Educational Needs Coordinator (SENCO) role to lead SEN across the school, interventions were my priority and these have become much more organised and ordered, with jurisdiction of whose role it is to organise and monitor much clearer. The monitoring of interventions systematically has been an important part of my school's action plan over the last year. There is now clear baseline and outcome data, as well as key information being recorded and reported back to class teachers, which in turn is ensuring interventions are becoming much more effective.

DOI: 10.4324/9781003466550-7

Like many schools in recent years, the number of our intervention groups has increased due to larger gaps in the children's learning from missed education and time away from the classrooms. Newton and Wilson (2011) suggest that quality first teaching needs to be given to the children who struggle the most, by the most qualified people – teachers. However, in our school, there were several teaching assistant-led (TA) support groups, but very few teacher-led support groups. These interventions and support groups usually took place after whole-class learning, often in the afternoon, once children had sat in class not understanding the learning from the start of a lesson.

After discussing the idea of having a focus on teacher-led interventions during a senior leadership team (SLT) meeting, I went away and spent time researching and looking into the importance of teacher-led interventions. I read articles and research papers, and found most helpful:

- Information published by the Education Endowment Foundation (EEF), where their guidance from 'Selecting Interventions' stated the importance of teaching quality and that it was optimal for delivery to be by a qualified teacher.
- Minkel's (2015) explanation that pre-teaching is more effective than reteaching, as it can transform the way a child sees themselves.

After spending time gathering information about teacher-led interventions, the idea I felt would be most beneficial to trial in my school was pre-teaching, led by the teacher.

As my starting point, I took Vetter et al.'s view (2020) that interventions to target numeracy and literacy skills are vitally important to boost progress and attainment, and that support for pupils who have difficulties in specific areas should be provided by the teacher, rather than a TA. With this focus, I based my action research project on providing teacher-led support and interventions carried out *before* the whole-class learning of maths lessons. I aimed to assess any impact this small-group support may have on confidence in the whole-class maths lessons and the academic attainment of six pupils from Year 5, who had stated they found maths difficult and lacked confidence to start learning activities without adult support.

Lalley and Miller (2006) explain that pre-teaching a concept, problem and computation significantly increases the overall achievement in maths, so I planned for our pre-teaching intervention to take place between 8.45–9.05am each morning for five weeks. This would support pupils' learning of the new topics that were being taught in the maths lesson that day. Taking another of Vetter et al.'s (2020) views that physically active sessions significantly improve learning compared with classroom conditions, I planned the sessions to be short and 'hands on', where pupils learnt the concepts or methods which could then be practiced and applied later in the classroom.

Collecting evidence to measure impact

Evidence collection

I used action research methods of observation and interviews to measure the impact of this intervention. These included working with and observing the pupils in group sessions, interviewing the teacher and pupils, and pupil questionnaires. This enabled me to be reflective on what we did, to understand and improve our practice.

- First, I gained consent from the Year 5 class teacher and interviewed her to discuss the pupils who had maths difficulties in the class. I wanted to understand what provisions were currently in place for these pupils, how they engaged and responded to daily maths lessons, as well as their current attainment. This interview included structured questions such as:
  - How do you know which children are finding maths difficult in the classroom?
  - What is currently in place for these children who find maths difficult?
  - What strategies do you find are the most effective to support these children?

  This was to ensure that certain topics were covered, however I wanted to keep it informal and flexible in style, allowing different ideas to emerge.

  After gaining consent from pupils and parents to take part, as BERA (2018) states is essential ethical practice, I interviewed the pupils. Again, this interview had some structured questions, for example: 'Do you enjoy maths?' and 'What do you find difficult in maths?' to ensure that some specific topics were covered, while also providing opportunities for them to be open about how they felt about maths, their maths learning and what they did to improve their learning. This was very informal, giving the pupils freedom to discuss their opinions and enable different ideas to emerge. I wanted all participants to feel at ease and relaxed.

I then gave them a questionnaire which contained statements like:

- I feel confident during maths lessons
- I always understand the maths lessons
- I can confidently start the learning as I know what to do
- I always ask for help if I am unsure

This enabled me to dive a little deeper into their learning in the classroom during maths, and compare these responses with their interviews. Each statement had four columns labelled 'Strongly Agree', 'Agree', 'Disagree' and 'Strongly Disagree'. The children were then able to tick the column they felt best suited. I also gave them the Year 5 decimals assessment sheet to collect baseline data as this was their next unit of learning.

- After collecting all this information, I carried out daily maths sessions each morning between 8.45–9.05am, before their maths lesson. In each session the pupils were pre-taught the key concepts and methods that they were going to be looking at during the maths lesson that day. I planned fun, hands-on activities, which involved using lots of resources the children could take back and use in the classroom. We tended not to use worksheets, taking photos of the activities we had completed instead. The resources included counters, base ten and bead strings. Field notes were made to document what happened during these daily small-group sessions – for five weeks. The sessions were carried out at a learning area in the school's studio.
- I had brief discussions with the pupils at the end of each week to gather their point of view on various aspects of their group sessions and their learning at the end of each week. Again, this discussion had some structured questions to ensure that certain topics were covered – for example, whether they enjoyed the sessions, what would make them better, what they had learned that helped them later in the classroom and what things were important for small-group work – but it was also informal

and flexible, allowing the pupils to develop their answers and extend their ideas.

- I carried out an interview with all the pupils as a group at the end of the five weeks to discover if their views on maths had changed from the start.

- Finally, I repeated the Year 5 end-of-block assessments that pupils had completed at the beginning of this intervention and researched on its impact, to compare the results with those at the start. This provided some quantitative evidence from data to complement the findings of the qualitative evidence from the interviews.

Impact

The findings from this research showed that the pre-teaching intervention was worthwhile and resulted in changes being implemented within school.

Teacher interviews

Having interviewed the teacher prior to the pre-teaching interventions, I felt assured that these pupils had already been having effective support. She told me:

> The children are currently having weekly interventions with the class TA to give them a little more support than some of their peers and give them a confidence boost.

She felt that the sessions provided:

> A relaxed environment where children could have some banter and enjoy themselves . . . it isn't a formal group, it's relaxed but . . . they're learning and being challenged.

She also stated that pupils listened and took on board what they were learning: she thought they responded enthusiastically.

Pupil initial interviews

When completing the initial interview with the six pupils, I was expecting them to say they enjoyed the interventions, as they sounded extremely effective and fun. However, the children stated that sometimes they found these maths booster sessions "too long" and "they can be boring". One of the children also stated, "We miss out on the fun stuff in Topic because we have to go out in the afternoon to do more maths."

This difference of perspectives made me realise, on reflection, it would have been extremely interesting to observe a few of the intervention sessions that the pupils were a part of before the pre-teaching sessions. It also made me realise that the pre-teaching sessions I was planning needed to stay short and be well paced, but also most importantly, be fun for the children and make them more excited about maths.

Pupil initial questionnaires

All six pupils in the initial questionnaire reported having negative feelings before or during math lessons. The most common word used by them was 'anxious' closely followed by 'nervous'. I understand there are times when everybody is nervous or anxious, however these are not the only feelings we want the pupils to have while they are at our school. Our school policy and vision statement states that all children are supported in a safe, inclusive environment where all can achieve. We want all pupils to have positive feelings about maths, even if it is an area that they find difficult.

All of the pupils ticked the 'Strongly Disagreed' box for the statement 'I always understand the maths lessons' and five out of the six children ticked that they disagreed with the statement 'I can confidently start the learning as I know what to do'. This made me realise how important it is that some pupils be given extra time to explore the new concepts or methods. Like many interventions, pupils tend to go over the concepts and methods they have struggled with once they have been taught it, rather than looking at it beforehand. During the explanation of the purpose of this intervention and what we would be doing, all six children were extremely excited about learning what they were going to be looking at in the lesson in advance, thriving off the idea that they would know before the rest of the class.

Pupil assessment

On the 'decimal assessment' sheet that was given to the pupils to complete in the first session, all six pupils scored less than 5/20. While completing the assessment all the pupils were very unsure and on most of the questions did not know where to start – often not even attempting the questions. One pupil scored 0/20, two scored 2/20, one scored 3/20 and two scored 4/20. I was expecting all the children to score low, as this was a new area of learning that they had not covered in Year 5 yet, however it was slightly concerning as they have looked at decimals in previous years at school. We did have a brief discussion after the assessment where they said they could not remember how to 'do decimals'.

Observations

Each morning, the pupils seemed excited and eager to attend the pre-teaching sessions on a daily basis, often checking with me when I was at the gate first thing in the mornings to make sure it was still happening. It was clear that they saw maths more positively and thought it was more fun.

In the sessions, we went through the key learning points, concepts and methods pupils would need for that day, using resources like counters, base ten and other objects to represent the learning. I could see that the pupils certainly felt more confident when using these objects to scaffold their learning. I worked closely with the class teacher to ensure that these objects were also available in the classroom for the pupils to use during lessons, which was extremely beneficial as at least three of the group collected these objects on a daily basis to help support their learning. This is something they had not done before, despite stating in their questionnaire at the beginning that they used resources in the classroom to help them.

Reflections

I found the weekly reflection time at the end of each session useful as I was able to see what pupils had found most beneficial each week and if there were activities they did not enjoy. As this intervention was to help support them, as well as boost their confidence and attainment, I wanted to ensure I was continually monitoring and improving it if there were ways to do so. Pupils identified these sessions were much more fun, comparing their sessions to ones they had with the TA in previous interventions. Certainly, there was an overwhelming feeling amongst them that the sessions were more enjoyable: "It doesn't feel like we are doing maths because it is so much fun" was a comment that was made multiple times by a child in the pre-teaching session.

Table 6.1 Comparison of pre-assessment and post-assessment results

Pupil	Pre-assessment Result	Post-assessment Result
A	0/20	12/20
B	4/20	14/20
C	2/20	13/20
D	3/20	16/20
E	0/20	12/20
F	4/20	17/20

Final results

All six pupils improved their score on the Year 5 end-of-block assessment they completed at the end of the five-week intervention. The following table (Table 6.1) shows pupil results in the decimal assessment that they completed at the start and end of the intervention.

All pupils felt a sense of achievement and were extremely pleased with what they had scored. They seemed to have a different attitude, and on the majority of the questions they got incorrect, they had persevered and had a go to try and answer them, unlike in the initial assessment.

At the end of the five weeks of these sessions, I used the final interview questions to gather the pupil's opinions and responses to the intervention. All six pupils reported that they felt they had improved their score because of the pre-teaching sessions each morning. All six also agreed that they preferred them being shorter sessions, but happening every day. Their feedback included:

> I like these sessions much more because I can use this work in the classroom when we do our maths lessons because it's the same work.

> I like knowing about the learning before the rest of the children in the class.

> I put my hand up much more now in the classroom because I know more of the answers.

> It makes maths easier for me and I want to keep doing it.

> I have learnt new things and I enjoy doing maths like this.

All pupils said these sessions were fun, enjoyable and agreed that maths is not as scary as they thought. Two pupils stated they still feel a little bit nervous about maths, but also excited.

When discussing these views with the class teacher, she also stated that she had seen a difference in the group, noting improvements in all six – of their progression, confidence and attainment. It was interesting when I asked the pupils if they thought pre-teaching sessions would help them in the future, they all stated "Yes" and also said they thought pre-teaching sessions should be used with pupils from other classes because "you learnt more".

Recommendations

Recommendations for practice

1. Teacher-led interventions
    After analysing the intervention data, interview feedback and results, it was evident that some changes needed to be made in our school, to ensure that interventions are effective. Taking as a starting point that interventions are *most* effective when delivered by teachers, this is an important area for us to pursue to ensure teachers are delivering as many interventions as possible to support pupils – whether they have difficulties in specific subjects like maths, or other wider learning needs. Teacher time is precious; however, it is vital to ensure we are providing the most effective provisions for these children to show progression and improve attainment. One way I have thought about doing this is by using assembly time in the mornings or allowing pupils to come to school slightly earlier so they start their intervention as other children are arriving at school.
2. Effective interventions
    During this research, points that arose which I thought important to highlight were:

    - Pupils seem to prefer short daily sessions, rather than longer weekly sessions.
    - Hands-on, physical activities were much more engaging than worksheets and ensured pupils are provided with resources to scaffold their learning when using later in class.

These points were discussed in a SLT meeting and then I shared them with teachers during a staff meeting. Teachers within the school are now taking this into account when planning, and are beginning to adapt their interventions. For example, as a school we have revisited ways to ensure our displays do not just become 'wallpaper' – they need to always be purposeful and supportive, and staff ensure resources are available for children, either on their desks ready to use or accessible for pupils to help themselves.

Recommendations for leading whole-school development

It is extremely important that as a member of our SLT, I select the right problem to focus on. As recommended by the EEF (2019: 12), 'Don't jump to considering new approaches to implement before rigorously examining the problem.'

Identify the problem

In this case study, I discussed my initial findings with the SLT, who agreed we needed to continue developing our interventions, as some were not effective because they did not have a sense of purpose. We considered that it can be difficult to see what progress had been made by pupils and that it was also impossible for teachers to lead all interventions, so there would be sessions which are delivered by TAs.

Recent reports, along with this research, has made me reflect on and rethink what TAs are expected to do in our school. As teachers, we have high expectations of pupils; we know their levels and understand what they need to do to improve. Due to the nature of their job and the way they spend their days, TAs do not always have this knowledge or insight. It was agreed that training was needed, and time has been provided for all the TAs to observe and work with other TAs in school who have had more experience teaching these groups or to share their knowledge with others. TAs are also encouraged to attend staff meetings and training sessions to develop their knowledge and understanding alongside the teaching staff.

Understand how new developments can impact staff

I need to develop an understanding of how often pre-teaching needs to occur, as I realise daily pre-teaching can be time consuming and is unsustainable in the long term, especially if the expectation is for all teachers to be completing this. If we do decide to go ahead with pre-teaching as a school-wide strategy, there needs to be consideration on what we can 'take off' staff, so their workload is not continually growing.

Interventions and parents

It is important to ensure parents are kept informed about interventions with children, because our parents were keen to find out how their children got on during the intervention. We as a school, with a lead from the SLT, must ensure that communication is happening and that time is allocated for all parties involved. This research has heightened the importance of communication; therefore we are changing the way we inform parents of their child's group work.

Recommended reading

Education Endowment Foundation. Available online at: https://educationendowmentfoundation.org.uk/.
This is an extremely useful website. It has a broad range of reports, research and evidence that will help improve teaching and learning. You will find anything and everything on here – it is now my 'go to' website!

Why I prefer pre-teaching to Remediation for struggling students (Minkel 2015)
I enjoyed reading this, it is a very quick read. The focus is all about the pupils and how providing them with a 'preview' of future lessons can totally transform their learning.

Effects of Pre-teaching and Re-teaching (Lalley and Miller 2006)
This was useful to consider the differences between pre-teaching and re-teaching, and helped me decide which intervention I thought would be the most beneficial for the pupils I was working with.

References

British Educational Research Association (BERA) (2018) *Ethical Guidelines for Educational Research*. London: BERA.
EEF (Education Endowment Foundation) (2019) *Guidance Report. Putting Evidence to Work: A School's Guide to Implementation*. Available online at: https://educationendowmentfoundation.org.uk/public/files/Publications/Implementation/EEF_Implementation_Guidance_Report_2019 (Accessed 28/01/2024).
EEF (Education Endowment Foundation) (n/a) *Selecting Targeted Interventions*. Available online at: https://educationendowmentfoundation.org.uk (Accessed 28/01/2024).

Lalley, J. and Miller, R. (2006) Effects of pre-teaching and re-teaching on math achievement and academic self-concept of students with low achievement in math. *Education*, 126(4): 747–755.

Minkel, J. (2015) *Why I Prefer Pre-Teaching to Remediation for Struggling Students*. Available online at: https://www.edweek.org/teaching-learning/opinion-why-i-prefer-pre-teaching-to-remediation-for-struggling-students/2015/ (Accessed 28/01/2024).

Newton, C. and Wilson, D. (2011) *Keys to Inclusion*. Nottingham: Inclusive Solutions UK Limited.

Vetter, M., O'Connor, H., O'Dwyer, N., Chau, J. and Orr, R. (2020) 'Maths on the move': effectiveness of physically-active lessons for learning maths and increasing physical activity in primary school students. *Journal of Science and Medicine in Sport*, 23(8): 735–739.

Chapter 7

Exclusion

The impact of limited wider-life experiences

Jemma Cotton

Context

My school is a primary school in an area of high deprivation with 221 pupils on roll, 128 pupils receiving pupil premium funding and 48 pupils on the Special Educational Needs and Disability (SEND) register, 25 of whom received additional funding. The demand for support with Social, Emotional and Mental Health (SEMH) has become the primary area of need. Over the years, the level of deprivation within our school community has risen and school staff have witnessed an increase of SEMH needs. Numerous interventions have been put in place to support the needs of pupils, but behaviour concerns have continued to rise significantly, with younger pupils displaying aggressive behaviours. As a school, we have acknowledged behaviours are used to communicate emotion and are often linked to either home life, social exclusion, or fear of failure. However, behaviours have become so extreme that staff are worried, and to some extent frightened, about working with certain pupils and integrating them back into the classroom.

I chose this project after observing one pupil in particular struggling to integrate within school, choosing to exclude herself from everyone. She refused to go into the classroom and consistently created stories of experiences at home, including going on an aeroplane overnight to Spain before returning to school the next morning. She used verbal and physical aggression to gain attention, which negatively impacted her social life in school and resulted in poor attendance.

I decided to explore how pupils with SEND are excluded at school due to limited wider-life experiences, which I am aware can lead to pupils being excluded socially and academically through

DOI: 10.4324/9781003466550-8

peer rejection. I looked closely at our most vulnerable pupils with SEND who had SEMH as their primary area of need. The pupils selected displayed persistent absences throughout the year. I looked at linking pupils' limited wider-life experiences and feelings of exclusion both in and outside the classroom, to identify how these could impact pupils socially and academically.

Throughout the project I worked alongside teaching staff and other professionals, including our pastoral team, to evaluate the importance of wider-life experiences, with a focus on how teachers can implement these daily within the curriculum to enhance pupils' social interaction, language development and academic progress.

Developing whole-school practice

In my opinion, a good leader inspires all stakeholders to achieve and succeed in an inclusive environment. Leadership challenges theory and practice to create shared values, visions, and growth to promote success. Bates and Bailey (2018) identified the 'Force Field Analysis' model by Kert Lewin (1935) to be a successful model when implementing and addressing the fear of change, as it allows the entire team to be involved with important decisions, reducing feelings of anxiety around change. At my school, staff have always been sceptical about change as often it resulted in failure and this was a belief I needed to overcome. Throughout the project I used a democratic style of leadership to promote creative and inclusive ideas from those involved, creating a collaborative approach.

Staff in school previously commented that the pupils displaying concerning behaviours often had limited wider-life experiences – both in and outside of school – causing them to feel neglected and embarrassed during activities. I decided to research links between limited wider-life experiences and exclusion in schools and found two useful studies:

- Taket et al. (2009) was a key piece of research. They identified nine areas closely associated with social exclusion. Seven of these were associated with living in disadvantaged areas, including poverty, low income, low socioeconomic status and socioeconomic disadvantage. They identified where a family does not provide high-quality dialogue and wider-life experiences, pupils lag in their learning potential, leading to social exclusion.

- The second piece of research was by the Alliance for Inclusive Education (ALLFIE 2020), which stated that the social model of disability should be applied in learning environments to prevent disabled students being excluded from activities and school life, especially as 'velcro' support can cause social isolation.

These linked closely with experiences identified by our teachers, whereby pupils with limited wider-life experiences and a lower-level vocabulary presented behaviours that excluded them from interactions in the classroom because of the learning activities set, rather than their ability.

I used an intervention programme which was conducted with five pupils from year groups three to five: all had SEND and SEMH as a primary need. Using a democratic style of leadership, I asked teachers to develop a bank of activities they believed would be beneficial when supporting the SEMH needs of pupils: this enabled staff to feel included in the project and take ownership over changes. It took place over a six-week block, with one 'wider-life experience' session a week and the option to take part in an additional boxing session after school each week. The wider-life experiences allowed pupils to focus on team building, social skills, self-esteem, and confidence. Sessions included an enterprise week, life skills, forest school, team building and sporting activities like bowling. The activities were displayed in classrooms and were discussed in class each week, enabling pupils involved in the study to engage in discussions.

Collecting evidence to measure impact

Evidence collection

Interviews

I started by asking the pupils and 14 teachers, who either taught or had previously taught the pupils involved, to complete a semi-structured interview. The teachers' interviews focused on the impact of wider-life experiences and their importance in a child's education, whilst the pupil interviews focused closely on their current experience in school. The pupils selected spent, on average, six out of ten sessions out of the class because of challenging behaviours or poor attendance. I used open-ended questions that could be adapted depending on the need of individuals in an informal setting so that pupils did not feel pressured. Johnson and Christensen (2012) state that open-ended questions allow pupils to use natural language and so provide high-quality information, and I found using these allowed pupils to elaborate on their thoughts regarding exclusion derived from limited wider-life experiences. I decided to record the interviews both on a form and using a voice recording app, so that I could analyse emotions in voices as views were portrayed.

Observations

I decided that observations would be the most valuable source to gather qualitative data as it is a method used in school daily. Pupils were observed twice every other week, with one observation taking place in the playground on the same day as their wider-life experience and one during class discussions linking to wider-life experiences, two days after their experience. Observations were used to triangulate evidence and analyse pupils socially and academically, whilst observing their verbal skills and body language. I was able to complete the observations in a nonintrusive way as I am regularly on the playground and in classrooms.

Questionnaires

At the end of the project, I used questionnaires with open-ended questions to identify the impact:

- Teachers were asked to review the impact that wider-life experience interventions had on the pupils involved, socially, emotionally, academically and in terms of their attendance.
- Pupils focused on their feelings surrounding the experiences, to discover whether providing wider-life experiences on a weekly basis reduced feelings of exclusion. I decided that questionnaires allowed the least intrusive approach to identify pupils' true emotions, promoting honesty using either written/pictorial responses, or voice recordings: the recording format was an individual choice.

School data

I used quantitative school data to measure the pupils' progress and attendance – analysing this before the intervention programme began and during its final week. This provided a triangulation of evidence with the qualitative data collected from pupil and staff views on the effectiveness of the programme – for example, to compare feelings of inclusion and school attendance and identify any links between feelings of inclusion and academic achievement levels. This created a snapshot of how increasing wider-life experiences could improve pupils' engagement and reduce exclusion, focusing particularly on social exclusion.

Ethics

In line with BERA (2018), informed consent was gained from teachers, pupils and their parents, before taking part in the study. They were made aware of confidentiality and understood that the results would be shared externally. All pupils were made aware of their right to withdraw.

To ensure that the impact of the intervention was measurable, I created a robust monitoring and evaluating (M&E) schedule whereby senior leaders and I collected pupil voice and observed interactions at least once a week. The information was discussed during leadership meetings. The information was collated with attendance and information data to provide a measurable impact.

Impact

Teachers

It is particularly important for pupils from disadvantaged backgrounds and vulnerable groups to be taught SEMH skills to strengthen their social and emotional skills and avoid developing a feeling of exclusion within the school environment. During interviews, teachers provided strong views about the background of the pupils in our school, including their limited access to their wider community, and a passion to improve their experiences. One stated:

> Pupils with SEMH needs lack the ability to transfer social skills into everyday experiences, which can exclude them from peer groups. Through providing them with practical activities such as pizza making, and den building children can work in a small group to develop their resilience which enhances their team building and social skills.

Staff have volunteered their own time to run clubs outside of school to support this need. When asked which experiences could be incorporated within school, one teacher suggested:

> Simple trips like a train ride. Buying an item from a shop.

These are experiences that we take for granted, however for many of the pupils at our school – not only those with SEND – such experiences are limited.

During the initial interviews it was evident that all teaching staff agreed that limited wider-life experiences do unintentionally exclude some pupils (including those with SEND) inside the classroom – as one teacher explained:

> When reading new texts, pupils have a huge lack of understanding of vocabulary due to their lack of wider-life experiences meaning they can't access the text to answer questions. This impacts pupils within the classroom as it links to everyday learning, yet pupils don't feel confident to participate in class and feel embarrassed, which excludes them from the school community.

When looking at the impact of our study, one teacher expressed the view:

> Pupils remain trapped in a bubble of limited opportunities resulting in them trying less in school as they aspire similar to those of their parents. If pupils see there is more to life than (catchment area name) then they will put in greater effort into academic studies to greaten their life chances and career progression.

This powerful quote reinforces the importance of wider-life experiences and the potential impact it can make within an individual's life.

Pupils

At the start of the programme, when pupils were asked to rate their experiences in school, they gave an average rating of 2.20 out of 5 stars for 'enjoyment of school'. This increased to an average rating of 4.40 after it had been completed, with all pupils stating that the wider-life activities made them feel happy and included. All pupils also identified that their confidence levels had increased within school, both in the classroom and socially, giving this an average rating of 4 out of 5 stars.

During the initial interview, pupils were asked what would make school better. They all responded with active ideas that would take place outside of the classroom, with four of the five pupils enjoying being able to socialise with peers who shared the same experiences and views as themselves, making them feel comfortable and included within their environment.

The observations identified ways in which changes took place for pupils during the programme. When observed inside the classroom and in the outdoor environment, pupils' body language was more expressive in the outdoor area with peers of a similar background to them. Pupil 5 asked for help and was observed taking risks that she would never have dreamed of doing before. Following this experience, she took a photograph and brought it into the classroom to show her class teacher, and was observed interacting with her peers as she told them what she had made. This became a memorable experience for Pupil 5. During the final stages of the research, she identified in her questionnaire that: "Using the drills and building my house" was one of her favourite parts – she felt included, her confidence had developed and her ability to communicate with her peers had increased. Similar observations were made for all five pupils, suggesting that the environment is significantly important when promoting inclusion within the classroom.

During the semi-structured interviews at the start of the study, pupils were asked what their favourite activity was to participate in at home. All their answers related to television and computerised gaming/interaction. There was little evidence of wider-life interactions and two admitted to making up an experience when talking to others. When asked why they did this, their answers related to social acceptance:

> I told Miss *** that I went to Skegness one weekend, because I wanted her to think I had fun.
>
> (Pupil 3)

Like I beat someone up because they picked on B. I didn't really, but I could have done because everyone wanted to get in a fight.

(Pupil 2)

Both responses suggested pupils desired to be positively accepted by others. Through creating make-believe experiences, they were able to engage with others in their immediate environment where others were interested in what they had to say.

Social rejection impacts significantly on pupils, leading them to significantly increase challenging and undesirable behaviours. Porter (2014) stated that teachers must lead peers to accept 'troubled' pupils and some of their behaviours to ensure full inclusion within the classroom: regaining a sense of belonging can lead pupils to increase academic ability, social integration and improve behaviours. We saw this happening. During the wider-life experience skills sessions, pupils began to display positive body language, and were not hesitant when discussing different situations. Pupil 3 even admitted to never participating in some of the experiences that were being discussed, rather than creating a make-believe situation.

All five pupils requested to continue their weekly wider-life experience intervention programme. They all identified ways in which the programme helped to support their progress within school. Tables 7.1–4 show direct quotes from pupils outlining how these experiences have helped to reduce the feelings of exclusion and promote their own independent progress.

Table 7.1 Feelings

How did the different activities make you feel?
Pupil 1	Fun, happy because I got to play games after. It makes me happy because I know that I have done an achievement. I got to show everyone, lots of people, what I could do.
Pupil 2	Feel good because it made me not feel so angry.
Pupil 3	I would release my anger when I had a bad day. We worked through stuff together and would run, it would help me not get angry because I wasn't thinking about things.
Pupil 4	Excited that I get to go to Superbowl with my friends and show them things.
Pupil 5	Feel happy, I like doing it.

Table 7.2 School environment

How have the different activities helped you around school?

Pupil 1	Helped me be good like to control my anger and stuff.
Pupil 2	It made me want to come to school and do boxing and see other people.
Pupil 3	Not as angry in school and I don't get in trouble as much. I like doing things with my friends.
Pupil 4	To be patient with them and to take things in turn sometimes.
Pupil 5	Helped me to do work. I do my work now.

Table 7.3 Social interaction

How have the activities helped you to communicate with your friends?

Pupil 1	Good, like I didn't used to talk about myself much because I didn't want to. I like talking to others about what I've got and what I can do. I go to the boxing club now as well, so I tell them that.
Pupil 2	I felt happier in school and stuff like I showed my friends punching and that.
Pupil 3	I like to show them what I've done in the group, and we copy it, but like I tell them what to do.
Pupil 4	I tell them how good I am and sometimes practise bowling together on the playground.
Pupil 5	I like to play with them and now they come in my room, and we can play with my things.

Table 7.4 Classroom engagement

How have the activities helped you within the classroom?

Pupil 1	Help me be good because I used to get frustrated and everything, now I don't so I can just tell my teacher or use what I have done.
Pupil 2	To be in school. I wanted to come in and I wasn't late on the days I did boxing.
Pupil 3	Using 5 steps of anger and take myself away now when I'm angry.
Pupil 4	Maybe I think to take it in turns.
Pupil 5	I do the work Miss gives me and sometimes I go in the classroom.

Table 7.5 Attendance and attainment data

Attendance July	Pupil 1		Pupil 2		Pupil 3		Pupil 4		Pupil 5	
	97%		61%		90%		72%		85%	
Attainment	May	July	May	July	May	July	May	July	May	July
Reading	BLW	BLW	OYG	OYG	INT	EXS	BLW	BLW	OYG	OYG
Writing	INT	BLW	OYG	OYG	OYG	INT	BLW	BLW	OYG	OYG
Maths	EXS	EXS	OYG	OYG	INT	EXS	BLW	EXS	OYG	BLW

Key: OYG – Other group level (-2years+); BLW – working below age-related expectations (ARE); INT – intervention, working slightly below ARE; EXS – exceeding ARE.

Pupils felt more confident following activities to speak in their classes and with peers, highlighting the importance of sharing needs of pupils with the class. As a result of sharing needs, pupils in the class asked those involved with the project more questions, which created social inclusion. An inclusive education allows inequalities in school to disappear. This small-scale study identified a strong link between happiness, confidence and inclusion when linked to social interaction, academic engagement and classroom inclusion. Through providing wider-life experiences focusing on team building and social skills to pupils on a regular basis, their confidence increased, impacting positively on contributions in discussions with peers and in class. The responses from pupils showed a positive influence on their school life impacting on their feelings, confidence, attendance, and academic progress.

Throughout the intervention programme pupils' attendance increased. Although over the six weeks of this research study their graded attainment levels did not always increase (as Table 7.5 shows), teachers did report that all pupils had made good progress in their learning.

Reflection on impact

Whilst research studies identify the connection between poverty, vocabulary and social exclusion to challenging behaviours, there is limited research into the impact of limited wider-life experiences in schools. Many of our pupils become excluded socially and academically as they experience peer rejection related to limited wider-life experiences. Rieser and Commonwealth Secretariat (2012) stated all schools should understand the processes of exclusion and restructuring to provide an inclusive education. My study identified a strong correlation between pupils experiencing wider-life experiences and their active involvement in school life. The more pupils engaged in activities, the more their challenging behaviours declined, as they developed a sense of belonging.

I believe strongly that more research is needed to guide educators in providing all pupils with high-quality wider-life experiences and strategies of how to implement these within the school setting to promote social and academic inclusion.

Recommendations

Recommendations for practice

- Ensure activities are inclusive for all pupils throughout the year to help those particularly with limited wider-life experiences and SEMH needs to feel included.
  Wider-life experiences reduced social exclusion of pupils as they provided pupils the opportunity to engage in discussions based on first-hand experiences. All pupils involved in the project explained how the activities enabled them to feel included.
- Teachers should dedicate specific time to teach all pupils explicit skills that will enhance and support their meta-cognitive strategies so they are able to develop in school socially. We noted that negative behaviours declined, the more pupils engaged with new experiences.
- Schools must identify personalised strategies to ensure all pupils develop a sense of belonging. Needs must be discussed with classes to create an inclusive and adaptive education setting for pupils with SEND, increasing all stakeholders' understanding of SEMH needs across schools.
- Teachers' planning should include planned activities that focus on team building and social skills, separate to topics, with time included for pupils to discuss experiences.
- Provide activities for pupils not based around academic subjects. This allows pupils to reflect on behaviours and identify strategies to support emotions, particular anger – our pupils developed new methods to support regulation.

Recommendations for leading whole-school development

- A democratic style of leadership should be used to create a collaborative approach and identify creative solutions when implementing wider-life experiences for all pupils.

  Using a collaborative approach with a whole staff 'buy in' focusing on the rationale will promote sustainability of approaches. Many staff are reluctant to change, but this is often because of the unknown: through being involved in a project alongside staff a collaborative approach is built as you are able to provide staff with integrity at all times by using first-hand experiences.

- Implementation must adapt to context over time. It needs a clear plan of monitoring and evaluation, with staff being able to contribute to the creation of systems – this will increase the success rate.

  Assigning staff to actions with timescales will support holding others to account. Through sharing findings with the SLT, school improvements can be identified.

- Being involved with the curriculum design will enable you as a SENDCo to be an advocate for pupils' needs and offer a valuable insight into inclusive strategies.

  This involvement will also allow you to challenge staff about their plans of providing wider-life experiences to ensure activities are planned with a focus linked to the curriculum. Using the curriculum design, plans can be made to observe behaviours surrounding activities and can be reviewed alongside data to highlight impact.

- Discussing needs and behaviours with pupils is critical to support inclusion within the school, but for this to happen staff need to understand pupils' backgrounds fully.

  Never assume that staff understand labels, and always take the time to thoroughly discuss pupils needs and coping mechanisms with each teacher.

Recommended reading

Taket, A., Crisp, B. R., Nevill, A., Lamaro, G., Graham, M. and Barter-Godfrey, S. (2009) *Theorising Social Exclusion*. Oxon: Routledge.
This book identifies ways to prevent exclusion by linking together a multiagency approach.

Bootman, G. (2023) *Independent Thinking on Being a SENCO*. Carmarthen: Independent Thinking Press.
This book provides simple ideas to supporting the SENDCo role in schools and ways in which to use your time effectively in management.

ALLFIE (The Alliance for Inclusive Education). Available online at: https://www.allfie.org.uk/.
This provides resources, advice and articles of voices from individuals with SEND to promote an inclusive education system.

References

ALLFIE (2020) *Making Things Happen; Young Disabled People; Amplifying Their Voices*. Available online at: https://www.allfie.org.uk (Accessed 29/01/2024).

Bates, B. and Bailey, A. (2018) *Educational Leadership Simplified: A Guide for Existing and Aspiring Leaders*. London: Sage Publications Ltd.

British Educational Research Association (2018) *Ethical Guidelines for Educational Research*. Birmingham: British Educational Research Association.

Johnson, R. and Christensen, L. B. (2012) *Educational Research: Quantitative, Qualitative, and Mixed Approaches*, 4th ed. Los Angeles: Sage Publications Ltd.

Porter, L. (2014) *Behaviour in Schools: Theory and Practice for Teachers*. Maidenhead, Berkshire: Open University Press.

Rieser, R. and Commonwealth Secretariat (2012) *Implementing Inclusive Education: A Commonwealth Guide to Implementing Article 24 of the UN Convention on the Rights of Persons with Disabilities*. London: Commonwealth Secretariat.

Taket, A., Crisp, B. R., Nevill, A., Lamaro, G., Graham, M. and Barter-Godfrey, S. (2009) *Theorising Social Exclusion*. London: Routledge.

Chapter 8

STRIDE

A step in the right direction for inclusion

Vanessa Mehta

Context

I work in a culturally diverse secondary school of 900 students; 136 students are eligible for Pupil Premium funding (UK government funding provided to schools to improve educational outcomes for disadvantaged pupils) and 89 are currently in receipt of free school meals. Currently, 20 students have Education Health Care Plans (17/20 are boys) and the total number of students on our Special Educational Needs Register is 96 (10.6%), which is below the current national average (12.2%). The increase in social, emotional, and mental health needs on the register is impacting negatively on school attendance.

I feel very passionate about inclusion, and in my role as Deputy Head (Pastoral), the Designated Safeguarding Lead (DSL) and Special Educational Needs Co-ordinator (SENCO), I realise the importance of this and agree with Glazzard et al.'s view that SENCOs hold the key to inclusion by promoting 'a philosophy of acceptance where all pupils are valued and treated with respect' (2015: 24). I want to have a positive impact on the inclusive ethos of my school setting, enabling me to voice the needs of disadvantaged students.

Barriers to learning can occur within interaction with any aspect of a school. They can be physical obstacles that cannot be avoided, or others like mental ill health or poverty. A circumstance or obstacle that keeps people apart prevents communication or progress. It was during a presentation on my National Award for SEN Co-ordination course that 'Poverty Proofing the School Day' (www. children-ne.org.uk) was highlighted. This had an aim to 'remove the barriers to learning which exist because of the impact of living in poverty' because students in these circumstances were 'stigmatised

DOI: 10.4324/9781003466550-9

repeatedly during the school day' (Mazzoli Smith and Todd 2016: 3). After a pilot project in the North East of England which carried out school audits using the perspectives of students, parents, and staff, it was discovered more than 30 common barriers to learning were experienced. This work was then developed into a national model that propagated best practices throughout schools, supported by a 'poverty proof toolkit' and school partnerships that shared the data and insights gathered. Schools involved reported that removing 'poverty barriers' helped to improve attendance, attainment and the student experience (Wardle 2022).

This all fuelled my passion regarding my research focus, as I have always strived to remove barriers to learning. I decided to adapt the 'poverty proofing model' to look at 'exclusion proofing' my school and investigate the barriers to attendance for our Year 7 boys who experience disadvantages in life.

How did students feel 'excluded' from certain school areas or events and practices during the school day, such as being part of the school community? I wanted to discover if students with SEND and/or mental ill health, or in situations of poverty, were experiencing barriers that affected their attendance, attainment and school experiences.

If a student attends school, they have an enhanced opportunity of progressing and achieving; ultimately they will reach their full potential. I hoped that findings from my research would lead to a whole-school strategy to improve attendance and ultimately improve achievement and students' experiences.

Developing whole-school practice

I have been a Deputy Head for 13 years, and the SENCO at my school for the last year. There is no legislation that insists SENCOs need to be a member of the senior leadership team (SLT), however the SEND Code of Practice does state, 'They [SENCOs] will be most effective in that role if they are part of the school leadership team' (DfE 2015: 6.87).

As a member of SLT I have a defined platform to articulate and disseminate the SEN values and vision with all stakeholders. I feel I have enabled inclusion to have a clear voice at SLT which ensures whole-school strategies are implemented effectively, in order to secure the expected progress for all. I see a huge part of my role is transforming strategic intent into action. This process is best outlined by Cheminais (2015: 35) as 'articulate, build, create and define'. My strategic view has ensured systems have been implemented with impact and definition. As Cheminais also says, one of the characteristics of an effective strategic leader is to challenge and question: I feel I relentlessly do this.

My leadership style is primarily democratic. I work best when collaborating. I enjoy building consensus. I really value the opinions of others, and use this to lead whatever initiative it may be. Leading people involves taking them with you. You have to be able to explain the rational reasons for the change, at least to the second level of 'why'. Understanding the currents of influence and power in the school, you have to be able to demonstrate that you are in control. You need the emotional maturity and insight to support people, stand up to them, and help them manage their emotional responses and your own:

> We should never, ever, ever underestimate the power we have as leaders either to do good or to do damage and we should always be sensitive to unintended consequences as a result of our leadership.
>
> (Munby 2018: 8)

Exclusion-proofing group

I selected ten male, Year 7 students to discover if they were experiencing any barriers in our school. I chose these because we had an increasing number of males struggling with mental health and feeling insecure at school. This in turn had led to poor attendance. I focused on exclusion proofing with boys who featured in one or more of the following groups:

- SEND
- Pupil Premium Funding
- Experiencing poverty

The common link for all the boys was social–emotional mental health concerns with low attendance. Pastorally, these students were discussed on a regular basis, and relevant interventions were in place. Despite various inputs from internal and external agencies to support them, all had attendance below the national average of 95% – see Table 8.1.

Table 8.1 Student attendance and support provided

Student	Attendance %	Attendance Post Pandemic	Support			Meeting Academic Targets
			SEND	FSM	PP	
A	85	↑	✓	✓	✓	✓
B	87	↑	✓			✓
C	79	↑	✓	✓	✓	
D	82	↑	✓	✓	✓	
E	83	↓		✓		
F	21	↓	✓	✓	✓	
G	85	↓	✓			✓
H	87	↑		✓	✓	✓
I	89	↑	✓			✓
J	89	↑			✓	✓

Collecting evidence to measure impact

Evidence collection

As the SENDCo, Deputy Head, and DSL, the students knew me well. Given the sensitivity of this small-scale research project, it was essential to conduct it within an ethic of respect and informed consent (BERA 2018). The students needed to feel comfortable, and understand that it was entirely their decision to take part. I explained the research project clearly, being honest and transparent about what would happen, who would see the information, that their names and details would be kept confidential, their information would be stored securely and that they had the right to withdraw at any time. I discussed everything with their parents, who were very reassured and supported the aims of the project. I also made it clear to each student that in the event of a safeguarding disclosure, I would need to follow the correct safeguarding protocol.

I used three methods of collecting evidence:

1. A 'word wall' was used in order to ascertain the views of the students with regards to their understanding of various terms associated with exclusion (e.g. not noticed and unwanted), and

inclusion (e.g. safe and part of a team). This was important as it gave clear evidence of the students' understanding of what was meant by the terms. It also allowed me to tailor the question- naire and interviews.

2. A questionnaire as part of an interview. I used questions sug- gested in the Index for Inclusion (Booth and Ainscow 2011) – see Figure 8.1. Pupils chose to do this alone, in small groups, or with a friend. I also allowed the pupils to choose the member of staff to work with for this – I felt because of my school roles that I might not have been the right person for them!

3. Photographs to see where the students felt safe/unsafe, are happy/unhappy, and their favourite place/time of the day/least favourite place/time of the day. This was extended to a mapping task (to look at the physical, social and learning environment of the school and where they felt included/excluded). They coded where they felt safe and/or included, green, and where they felt unsafe and/or excluded, red.

Question: Please tick (✓) one response	Yes	Sometimes	No
Do you look forward to coming to school?			
I am happy at school			
I have good friends at school			
I feel part of a big community at school			
The school and the playground look attractive			
I feel safe in the toilets and playground			
I have some good friends			
I like my teachers			
The school helps me to feel good about myself			
The school helps me to feel good about the future			
I eat healthily at school			
Do you eat breakfast before coming to school?			
There is a comfortable place inside the school I can go to at lunchtimes			

Figure 8.1 Student questionnaire.

Question: Please tick (✓) one response	Yes	Sometimes	No
Children do not look down on others because of what they wear			
Boys and girls get on well together			
Disabled children are respected and accepted			
Children are kind to each other at school			
Adults are kind to children at school			
Children avoid calling each other hurtful names			
If anyone bullied me or anyone else, I would tell a teacher			
Teachers do not have favourites among the children			
If I have been away for a day a teacher wants to know where I have been			
If I have a problem, I can ask an adult for help			
I enjoy most of my lessons			
My work is displayed on the walls in the school			
I like to tell my family what I have done at school			

Please circle your responses:

1. How do you travel to school?
   Bus   Car   Walk   Cycle   Other (please specify)
2. Do you have any family activities?   **Yes   No**
   If yes, what do you family activities include?
3. Do you attend any afterschool clubs?   **Yes   No**
   If yes, what afterschool activities do you do?

Figure 8.1 (Continued)

I ensured that I revisited questions with the pupils within these different tasks to make sure responses given were still in line with their initial response.

Prior to collecting this evidence, I discussed where and how we would conduct the various tasks with the students to ensure they felt comfortable and would be very much involved in the set-up stage of the research. Interestingly, they chose to do the questionnaires individually, but liked the idea of taking the photographs and completing the mapping exercise in small groups; again, they chose who they did this with.

I found the time spent with the students fascinating. I thanked the students for their cooperation and maturity. We celebrated with hot chocolate! All the students apart from one were keen to know the outcome of my research.

Impact

Word wall

Every student understood the meanings of most of the terms on the word wall. They rapidly chose terms associated with how they felt. In some cases this was extremely sad because the students were less eager and willing to explain why they felt that way. Their responses were:

Student A – rejected, anxious, loved
Student B – not noticed, rejected
Student C – anxious
Student D – anxious, unhappy
Student E – happy, feel loved
Student F – did not want to engage with this task
Student G – anxious, unhappy
Student H – unhappy, forgotten
Student I – anxious, part of a team, loved
Student J – rejected, not loved, not wanted

The impact of the word wall enabled me to have a much clearer vision and understanding of each student with regards to how they felt about themselves.

Questionnaire/interviews

The students elected to do the questionnaire/interview individually. This made them more confident and comfortable about opening up, which enabled me to gain an insight into their individual struggles very quickly. Some common themes arose:

- Most of the students had experienced 'exclusion' at unstructured times and on nonuniform days.
- A significant number felt excluded from after-school conversations as they did not have access to social media.
- All talked about their work not being displayed on the walls in the school.

It was very apparent they were used to exclusion rather than inclusion and this appeared to have a negative impact on them. Only a minority could talk about any family activities, and even fewer attended after-school clubs. On a positive note, most of the students looked forward to coming to school, had friends, had a comfortable place to go at lunchtime, and ate breakfast. The students were positive about the teachers and how the teachers made them feel and supported them.

However, the students revealed some concerning things.

1. Student J talked about feeling rejected and that his parents did not love or want him. He said he was "sort of happy" at home but not happy at school as he struggled to learn:

    Learning is difficult for me, all my friends understand the work. I'm known as the joker as I misbehaved to avoid the work. I want to improve. I want to be happy. I want people to be proud of me.

    *As a result of this discussion, we arranged an emergency annual review. The student is now benefitting from some alternative provisions that support his needs.

2. Student H disclosed that he struggled to get into school on time because:

    I need to make sure my youngest siblings are dressed fed and in school. I'm happy in school but generally quite tired and exhausted at times.

    *We immediately referred the family for external support.

3. Student F was the most difficult to engage with and expressed the most negative views:

    I hate school. I will not attend. I do not know what I want to do in the future. I have no aspirations.

    My tutors in the home are good. I'm going out on walks.

    I have no real friends except one really good friend. I know this friend from my online gaming.

    *This last comment raised concerns for us and an early help referral was made with immediate effect.

4. Student I talked about his struggles in accepting his autism, but he now has good friends who accept him more and he felt that this would support his attendance. He spoke openly about his dislike of nonuniform days because "I have no good clothes to wear".

5. Student G spoke of being "anxious and unhappy". This appeared to be due to a lack of praise, both at home and in school. When I praised him for his maturity during the task, it was clearly appreciated.

    *I think is something we all need to reflect on. We can and should always try to find something positive to say regarding feedback. This can make a huge difference to the motivation and confidence of someone.

6. Student B's responses were upsetting to hear: he felt "lost", "not loved", "rejected".

Photographs

We met as a group to do the 'mapping the landscape' task and take photographs of where students felt happy/included/safe and unhappy/excluded/anxious.

Most of the students described feeling unhappy and excluded in the corridors, toilets, in the maths and computer studies building, and the food outlet queues. They coded these areas red. Student G in particular felt very strongly about the hall and the science labs making him feel excluded and anxious, so coded them red. The issue with the science labs was his fear of blood. He reported: "I feel anxious in these areas of the school. I hate the feeling of being around a lot of people".

All the students identified the 'SEND' and pastoral building, the Study Centre and the open plan toilets as 'green' during the mapping the landscape task.

While we have tried extremely hard to promote and ensure there is an inclusive and supportive ethos at our school, our aim must now be to turn the red (excluded) areas into green (included) areas.

Next steps

It was a pleasure to work with the students and start to understand the barriers to learning that they faced. We used the findings from this pilot work similarly with other groups on a rolling whole-school programme so that we could implement changes to better support students and improve their overall attendance. We have decided that a 'STRIDE' room will play a pivotal role in this as a step in the right direction for inclusion.

The vision for this STRIDE room includes involving staff with a clear understanding of SEMH and ensuring the students have an individualised plan and timetable which will focus on 'support towards resilience, independence, development and emotional intelligence' (STRIDE). My vision is that the STRIDE room will either act as a lever to ensure alternative provision is in place where necessary, or will be *a step in the right direction for inclusion back into mainstream education*.

Recommendations

Recommendations for practice

Understand the barriers to attendance for those who experience disadvantages in life

Understanding the difference between data and evidence is key to becoming an evidence-based practitioner because data is 'inert' information until evidence explains it (Wilkinson 2017; Jones 2018). Listening to students' descriptions of poverty and the impacts on schooling is an essential aspect of better understanding these nonmaterial aspects of poverty and their ramifications for all involved. I felt very strongly that, as the SENCo, I had a duty to attempt to discover what these barriers to learning were and to resolve them. I reflected on what the barriers are from individuals' perspectives, including the impact they have on attendance. Why do they not feel included? Only when we provide time to listen, and acknowledge the views of young people, will we truly understand the impact, and can then respond to this, *because inclusion is everyone's responsibility*.

The findings from my small-scale research project provided the basis for a development action plan which involved the following practices which I recommend to other schools:

1. We conducted a similar exercise, using interviews/question-naires, photographs and a 'word wall' with small cohorts of other identified potentially vulnerable students to provide them with a significant platform to be heard, so that we could understand any barriers that they faced.
2. We explored how to provide solutions to overcome the barriers described by the students. These included: i) providing students with an opportunity to purchase second-hand prom outfits (which received incredible support from parents and students); ii) – *discrete* provision of school uniform when it was found that pupils would not accept this otherwise; and iii) reducing the number of non-uniform days.
3. Our Pastoral team 'mapped the landscape', with the remit of focusing on bullying and sexual harassment. This identified areas where students felt vulnerable, so staff duty points have been reassigned. Some of these students now support the Pastoral Team in improving our support regarding bullying and sexual harassment.

Recommendations for leading whole-school development

As a school, our ultimate goal is for inclusion to be a 'given', regardless of the starting point. Ensuring we 'exclusion proof' to the best of our ability will eliminate barriers to learning. To do this we must listen and provide students with the opportunity to express how they are feeling, and show that by listening, wherever possible, we will improve the situation. Collecting students' views involved very little work to set up – it is incredible to think that a map and some photographs can have such an impact on change, and in this case, inclusivity.

In order to lead a whole-school development it is essential to ensure the majority of staff are on board. Staff need: i) clarity and reassurance of commitment; and ii) predicted progress and outcomes. Staff also need to know that it is not a bolt-on initiative, but a way of working that will lead to support and improvements for all.

Initially some staff were rightly pessimistic as they saw this as a bolt-on initiative. To try to change this view, we encouraged staff to visit the STRIDE room to see the students. Some students had not managed to return to school following the pandemic or as a result of SEMH. What the staff saw was these students in a learning environment being well cared for, supported and included. Staff who saw the positives then started to speak to other colleagues about this.

Staff were also really appreciative regarding the STRIDE room acting as a lever to explore alternative educational provisions for those students where STRIDE could not help. This also encouraged staff to become more optimistic about the positive impact of providing and using *evidence* in supporting students requiring alternative provision in order to learn and achieve their potential.

Recommended reading

Bates, B. and Bailey, A. (2018) *Educational Leadership Simplified: A Guide for Existing and Aspiring Leaders*. London: Sage Publications Ltd.
Easy to read! Very clear concepts and examples to implement as part of your leadership role. It also touches on equality and diversity.

Mason, M. (2005) *Incurably Human*. Nottingham: Inclusive Solutions.
This book clearly outlines and describes what it feels like to be excluded. It makes you realise why it is so important for students to be included in mainstream schools, regardless of the challenges.

References

Booth, T. and Ainscow, M. (2011) *Index for Inclusion: Developing Learning and Participation in Schools*. Bristol: CSIE.
British Educational Research Association (2018) *Ethical Guidelines for Education Research*. London: BERA.
Cheminais, R. (2015) *Handbook for SENDCOs*, 2nd ed. London: Sage Publications Ltd.

Department for Education and Department of Health and Social Care (2015) *Special Educational Needs and Disability: Code of Practice: 0–25 Years.* Available online at: https://www.gov.uk (Accessed 22/03/2024).

Glazzard, J., Stokoe, J., Hughes, J., Netherwood, A. and Neve, L. (2015) *Teaching and Supporting Children with Special Educational Needs and Disabilities in Primary Schools,* 2nd ed. London: Sage Publications Ltd.

Jones, G. (2018) *Evidence-Based Leadership and Management: A Practical Guide.* London: Sage Publications Ltd.

Mazzoli Smith, L. and Todd, L. (2016) *Poverty Proofing the School Day: Evaluation and Development Report, Project Report.* Newcastle upon Tyne: Research Centre for Learning and Teaching, Newcastle University.

Munby, S. (2018) *Principled Leadership in Challenging Times.* Available online at: www.bastow.vic.edu.au (Accessed 10/01/2024).

Wardle, C. (2020/2022) What are you waiting for? Get your school poverty proofed: Breaking the cycle of disadvantage. In Richards, G. and Wheatley, C. (Eds.), *Innovative School Leadership: Transforming Practices.* Abingdon: Routledge.

Wilkinson, D. (2017/2018) What's the difference between data and evidence? Evidence-based practice. In Jones, G. (Ed.), *Evidence-based Leadership and Management: A Practical Guide.* London: Sage Publications Ltd.

Chapter 9

Whole-school referral for SEND support

Katie Hawksley

Context

I am currently working as the SENDCO in a large mainstream secondary school in the East Midlands, which serves a broad demographic of children from surrounding communities. During my time at the school, I have worked as a pastoral lead and a teaching assistant, before becoming the Assistant SENCO in 2022 and moving to the SENDCO role in 2024. Our SEND (special educational needs and disabilities) team is made up of the Team Director for SEND and Safeguarding, and the SENDCO, who jointly oversee a team of five lead teaching assistants, four regular teaching assistants, a healthcare team, and apprentice teaching assistants who train with us regularly. We are fortunate to have teaching assistants specialising in areas such as physical and sensory needs, communication and interaction, social–emotional mental health, literacy and autism, as well as a healthcare team to further support with physical needs: these roles have been developed in support of our students and their needs.

As part of my Assistant SENCO role, I was given the opportunity to take part in a SENCO strategic leadership project alongside the SENCO, where we had to identify what could be developed to support whole-school best practice. When I took on the role of Assistant SENCO, I started to lead on exam arrangements, collecting information from teachers on how students work in their classes to inform changes needed to make exams accessible for all. During this process, I started to recognise that there was no clear way of teachers recording concerns and raising issues with the SENCO around exams and started to look wider at how we received information from teachers regarding our students.

DOI: 10.4324/9781003466550-10

Developing whole-school practice

During my first year, my role revolved around the paperwork side of being a SENCO, so when the opportunity came up for me to take part in a strategic leadership project alongside other SENCOs, my school thought this was a great opportunity to develop my strategic thinking and leadership skills. Since the areas I was working on highlighting the importance of communication with class teachers, I decided to focus on and create a simple referral process where teachers could pass on information to our team based on their own concerns, or to be used when their own quality first teaching and reasonable adjustments had not seen progress in line with other students in the classroom.

I wanted to look at how we get information from teachers and how this informs our involvement as the team who support students with special educational needs. I thought that although we had a graduated approach already established, there was a smoother way for this information to be raised with myself and the SENCO, without relying on emails and corridor conversations. This also applied to the pastoral team at school, who were often the first point of contact for parents/carers and students, and would contact us with initial concerns. Recently, we have seen more students accessing provision that is additional to, or different from, the universal provision offered, therefore the need for a streamlined process has become even more necessary.

Previously, staff didn't have easy ways to communicate or record concerns to ensure that they were picked up by the SENCO. I developed the referral form to enable teachers and pastoral staff to communicate concerns, even if they were to seek out low-level support or to make record of a concern that may form part of a bigger picture, similar to the robust safeguarding processes already in place, but for SEND. Without early identification and appropriate pathways for teachers to raise concerns, we become reactive to parent concerns after meetings with teachers or pastoral staff, or working backwards when a parent raises concerns of their own. By opening communication with all staff that was direct and didn't rely on trying to catch each other in the corridor or find each other in an office, the wider special educational needs team and I could respond to and log concerns for students with additional needs, or follow up on those who were suspected to have additional needs.

Designing the initial referral form

I started by thinking about what I would want to know if I was looking at the information without any knowledge of the student already, and starting to think about next steps. I thought about what I would want teachers to have done first before the referral was submitted and what we could offer as a team, following the referral. This led to the following decisions:

1. All students in our school who are categorised as 'SEN support' (accessing something additional to or different from the universal support and teaching available to all students) have a pupil passport that is available for all staff to see. These 'pupil passports' detail the student's diagnosis, strengths and needs, as well as recommendations made by the SENCO, teaching assistants, other professionals, students, and the parent/carer that will support the student to engage in learning to the best of their ability. So, a key question posed to staff in this form was: 'Have you accessed the student's pupil passport to look at their diagnosis/needs/strategies?' – to ensure that this first step of our school's process had been taken.

2. Our school emphasises quality first teaching as the first step in responding to pupils who have (or may have) SEN, so teachers were asked to: a) list the reasonable adjustments they had made to support the student's needs in the classroom, and b) detail the impact that quality first teaching had made. I felt that the form embedded 'responsibilities for SEN within a whole school approach, and to support all teachers to engage much more fully and effectively in fulfilling their statutory responsibilities' (Ekins 2015). This ensured that we had evidence of existing strategies and reasonable adjustments already trialled with the student, so that we could work from this stage and build on work already done. It prevented us from duplicating work, but also acknowledged the expertise of the teacher.

To formulate the rest of the form, I put together a framework that could be built upon once I had met with the wider SEND team. I then met with the team of teaching assistants, and we highlighted areas of concern that might be raised by teaching or pastoral staff, categorising concerns into the following:

- Communication and interaction
- Sensory and/or physical needs

- Autism
- Social–emotional mental health
- Cognition and learning
- Dyslexic traits
- Access arrangements for exams
- Classroom engagements
- Alternative learning space referral

We thought about the areas we could support based on our current team, as well as concerns where we knew we could access external support. I asked the team what we already offered to teachers to support students in their classes or pastorally and what they felt confident in providing. This identified:

- Meeting with members of the SEND team to discuss needs in detail.
- Classroom observations with the SEND team to provide additional strategies.
- Intervention based on the referral (with contact home and follow-up review).
- Dyslexia screenings.
- Access arrangements testing.
- Time-out pass/learning manager pass.
- Access to alternative learning environments in school.

We also discussed the importance of asking the teacher how long their concern had been present, and for clear details of the concern raised.

Collecting evidence to measure impact

Collecting evidence

Within the first year of the form being set up, we had 140 referrals from staff across the school asking for additional support from our team. We did receive emails about concerns, but continually directed staff to the referral form to ensure that this was the standard process we followed throughout the school. This support was mostly requested to support with student mental health and access arrangements testing for exams. To review this, I went through the form weekly and allocated tasks out to the team – however this became difficult with other deadlines and priorities, so I looked to create a better system for the following year.

After speaking to the SEND team, I learned that they felt the referral form has enabled better ways of us tracking and managing how concerns come to us as a team. The HLTAs manage their section of the form directly, which was preferred. It allowed them to see the source of a concern and discuss this directly with the staff member raising it, as opposed to this being communicated through an additional person. The HLTAs then feedback to both myself and the staff member who completed the referral so that they are aware of the actions taken following the concern. Within our own team, all SEND staff still use the HLTA referral form to ensure that we are all also following the process expected to be followed by other staff in the school.

The SEND team did raise that they feel the form is only as good as the person filling it in. This made me think about whether there should be training provided to staff on how the form can be used most effectively to inform the graduated approach, because assessment and the recording process is every teacher's responsibility (Cowne et al. 2015). Although training had been given around what the form was for and how to access this, I now think we should consider: a) how staff interact with the form; and b) how to get the best out of it in order to ensure the right support is implemented.

Support staff also said that these referrals allow them to request involvement for students who may have exhausted the support available from a pastoral perspective and may be in need of the more specialist support our team can offer. As a result, we have written this as part of a clear pathway for the pastoral team to follow, so it is clear how they can access support as part of the graduated approach for students, exploring the diagnostic pathway for ASD or ADHD, or for those with emotional needs.

Impact

Upon reflection, I felt that the referral for access to an alternative learning space was not comprehensive enough and did not provide sufficient evidence of the graduated approach through our pastoral pathway – students were not offered interventions targeted to specific barriers in the first instance and some students had been offered 'passes' to access the alternative learning space where another solution could have been implemented or trialled. Often, because referral for access to an alternative learning space was an additional aspect of the main referral form, the depth of this referral seemed an afterthought and the reason for it unclear.

Many of the students who had been accessing the alternative learning space were referred without a reintegration plan in place as to how we could support them accessing their mainstream provision again. I decided that a more comprehensive referral process was needed so that it was clear who would manage the provision and ensure that a reintegration plan was in place. Due to the removal of our 'reset' room which served as a place to support students with emotional needs, all our support has been re-centred to the alternative learning space in school. This has been overseen by me and the pastoral team leader who have been working collaboratively over the past year to improve this provision. We review referrals every two weeks and will often now follow these up with questions directed towards those filling out the referral form (often our pastoral team or year group leads) as to what they hope the referral will achieve or how the intervention will support with the barrier(s) experienced by the student directly. This has allowed us to redirect support to the most appropriate place.

Looking back at the referrals we had, some of the exam concerns were submitted with the assumption that a referral meant that we could grant a student extra time in exams or provide them with a scribe due to lack of training around access arrangements. It became clear that the expectations of the outcomes of the form had not been made clear and the process for exam concerns needed to be further reviewed.

This all led to my decision to break up the referral form into three separate forms to better manage the information coming to the team. These were divided into:

- Alternative learning space referral form
- Lead TA referral form
- Exam concerns referral form

A different team of people has become responsible for each form to ensure that we can act quickly in picking up these referrals and completing our 'section' of the graduated approach.

Alternative learning space referral form

The pastoral team lead and I manage the alternative learning space referral form which we review every Friday, ready for the upcoming week. This form asks the staff member about the aims of using the provision, how students will access work from the space provided and how many hours they will attend the provision. If we feel there isn't sufficient evidence or there are other ways to support with this need, we will suggest other steps as part of the graduated approach. This form, although accounting for the least number of referrals, is the most time consuming and needs the most monitoring, and so is overseen by team leaders in relevant areas.

Lead TA referral form

As mentioned previously, we have a team of lead teaching assistants who have their own areas of expertise. As part of their role this year, they have taken on the responsibility of managing the referrals for additional support in their own areas and offering their expertise to provide further strategies and assessments that will support both students and teachers in the classroom. Each week, these lead TAs meet and allocate referrals to the most appropriate member of staff, tracking this and feeding back to both the parent/carer and the teacher who initially completed the referral. In the past three months, 28 referrals have been made to the team and support has been offered. If there is little progress from this intervention and the student still shows a lack of progress in the area identified, this is raised with me or the SENCO to seek out further guidance or to start considering how we might gain the support of external agencies.

Exam concerns referral form

This form is managed by me, as the staff member who oversees access arrangements for exams, in collaboration with the teaching assistant who has the relevant testing qualifications so that they are able to carry out the correct tests. We have provided CPD for staff in school to better understand this process and what these needs may look like in the classroom. We review these referrals as and when they are submitted, so that we are able to keep on top of the referrals and paperwork associated with this process.

Recommendations

Recommendations for practice

- Make a referral form easy to access and provide training on how it should be used to get the best outcome.

  Overall, this process has had a positive impact on keeping our team and teachers in school accountable for their role in the graduated approach, where support becomes more specialised the further it is referred onwards. In the past few months, the forms have been added to our staff home page, which has made it easier for staff to access and know where they can be found. I feel that we are no longer working reactively, but proactively where the referral is raised in a timely manner.

- **Early identification.**

Reflecting on the project led me to think about the importance of early identification of additional needs and how the earlier we are able to put in place strategies to support students, the better progress will be made. Over the next year, I intend to put in place accompanying training for staff on the process for other areas of need, such as autism and ADHD where staff are often not as confident in reporting concerns of this nature.

- **Decide what kind of referral form is most relevant for you.**

I would recommend to other SENCO leaders considering a whole-school referral system to decide what kind of referral form would be most relevant for you and your setting, taking into account what type of requests you are receiving most from your pastoral team and teaching staff. The form should cater for what you can offer as an individual or as a team, while also considering what other resources you should be also offering to teachers and students. This could include any resources you can access externally, or training that you can access to meet the needs of your cohort.

Regardless of what you offer, I would always recommend that you ask staff to use the form to record what they did *first*, as this provides you with more context and lets you see what has already been trialled, so that you are accurately building on a pre-existing intervention and following the graduated approach. If there is one area in particular requested often on this form that you don't currently have access to internally, using this form as a case for training to be sourced for staff can be useful, as there is clear documented need for your school to have easy access to this resource.

Recommendations for leading whole-school development

The leadership project highlighted to me the need to be critical of my school and my own practice to ensure that processes are fit for purpose and meet the changing demands of our parents and students. You have to be willing to change these processes and design something that works well for you and your school. These need to be flexible – as a result of staff changes, I will continue to look at what we offer, to determine whether this still aligns with the expertise of my team, myself and the access we have to external services to support us. We must also be alert to ensure that further training is offered in response to the referral forms so that existing and new staff have the skills to raise all concerns that we might see from our young people.

Recommended reading

Ekins, A. (2015) *The Changing Face of Special Educational Needs Impact and Implications for SENCOs, Teachers and Their Schools*. London: Routledge.

I feel there needs to be more emphasis on collaboration and SEND being a whole-school responsibility. After reading this, I thought more about my role as a teacher and how I have a duty to contribute towards the early identification of any additional needs to ensure that pupils get the support they need. I know that, being both the SENDCO and a teacher, I have the skills to do this, but upon reflection this made me consider whether our team have provided teachers with the skills and training to follow the graduated approach. I think this is worth a read for anyone trying to support and upskill teachers in a large setting.

Aubin, G. (2022) *The Lone SENDCO: Questions and Answers for the Busy SENDCO*. Melton, Woodbridge: John Catt.

When I first started my role as Assistant SENDCO in 2022, I had so many questions and ambitions about how we could improve our SEND provision but wasn't sure where to look for these answers. I didn't have many friends in the profession and felt I didn't quite know how to access information of what this looked like in other schools. I saw this book recommended in an online group of SENDCOs and bought it – it has given me so many good pointers for what I should be doing and how we could develop our current practice. There are also lots of resources and QR codes within the book to directly support setting up assessment tools, specifically referencing how we use the graduated approach.

Example: neurodiversity referral form

The referral form will take approximately 5 minutes to complete. It will be used for you to access further support from the SEND team. Every week, we will meet and ensure that the information given on this form will be given to the right members of staff to offer support or put in place an intervention in response to your concern. We will feedback to yourselves the plan of action following your referral.

Question	Response
Staff Name	
Student Name	
Have you accessed the provision map for this student to look at their diagnosis/needs/strategies?	• Yes • No
My concern is about ...	• Communication and Interaction • Sensory and/or physical needs • Autism • Social Emotional Mental Health • Dyslexic Traits • Access Arrangements for Exams • Cognition and Learning • Alternative Learning Space Referral • Classroom Engagement
How long has your concern been present?	
Please provide details of your concern.	
If you are a teacher, how has quality first teaching had an impact? What reasonable adjustments have already been made?	
If you are a pastoral manager, what interventions have already been trialled with the student? What impact has this had on the student?	
Has there been any contact home that we should know about beforehand?	
What is the expected outcome of this referral?	• Meeting with the SEND team about student needs in detail • Intervention based on referral (with review and follow up meeting) • Further assessment of need facilitated by the SEND team • Access Arrangements Testing • Dyslexia Screening • Classroom Observation – SEN Classroom Review (if you are a pastoral manager, please discuss with teacher beforehand) • Access to an Alternative Learning Space in School • Time Out Pass

(continued)

(Continued)

Question	Response
Is there any safeguarding history that we should be aware of?	
If you are making a referral for a student to access an alternative learning space, please answer the following questions to ensure that we have all the relevant information to allow for a successful intervention. • What has led to an alternative space being needed? • What has been trialled before this referral? • How will the student access education from this space? Who will oversee this? • What is the long term plan for the student?	

References

Cowne, E., Frankl, C. and Greschel, L. (2015) *SENCO Handbook: Leading and Managing a Whole School Approach*. London: Routledge.

Ekins, A. (2015) *The Changing Face of Special Educational Needs Impact and Implications for SENCOs, Teachers and Their Schools*. London: Routledge.

Chapter 10

SEND policy and whole-school practice

What are staff doing and what do they know?

Michaela Brown

Context

Our school is a large primary school, with 630 children aged 4 – 11. We have an equal divide of boys and girls. The school has 11% (69 children) who receive free school meals, 10% with special educational needs (64 children), 7% pupils whose first language is not English, and 20% from minority groups. Our Key Stage 2 results are just above the national average, although progress scores are below the national average. Our school was created from an amalgamation of an infant and junior school, and four years after opening we had our Ofsted (Office for Standards in Education) inspection which graded us as a 'good' school in all areas.

Developing whole-school practice

Has recent legislation or school policy influenced me in my role, I ask? On a day-to-day basis, I don't believe it does, I certainly don't refer to the Code of Practice (DfE and DoH 2015) before meetings. However, when I hold staff meetings about provision or have tricky conversations with colleagues about improving support in their class, I need policy to back me up. When I meet with governors, I report on the steps we have taken at school, review our action plan, report on training, review numbers of children and their needs and how we meet them. Governors refer to our school policy and government guidelines to challenge my decisions and approaches.

But what does influence my daily practice? Values, experience, being a mother or the 'moral purpose' that leadership speakers (Fullan 2020) talk about? It needs exploring, unpicking, as it is this

DOI: 10.4324/9781003466550-11

influence that keeps me getting up in the morning. This influence is without doubt what sets and ensures the expectations and standards I set for our team's practice and that of my own.

At our school we have had four SENCOs in as many years. I took on this role to 'mind' it short term but have since fallen in love with the range of influences it has across school and the contact with parents and families. I am also the Deputy Head Teacher and Pastoral and Designated Safeguarding Lead. Our school has undergone change through collaboration to amalgamation, from a two-form entry to three over two sites, and then there was a pandemic. I cannot understate the difficulty of the challenges faced in bringing together two teams, two cultures and two different systems during all this change. Is this where policy is of importance or are values systems needed to ensure quality provision?

I find being a SENCO difficult. It is a constant battle to advocate for children and their families and as Curran, Moloney and Boddison question in their SENCO workload review, 'How is it fair on SENCOs to expect the 'same' depth and breadth of effectiveness . . . in the midst of this turmoil?' (Curran *et al.* 2018: 2). The turmoil they refer to is the demands on school budgets, the reduction of support staff and teaching assistants, the demand on SENCOs' time and dwindling specialist help. In addition, the SEND Review Green Paper states that navigating SEND systems is not a positive experience for children and their families, and that those with access to financial and social resources are often better placed to navigate the system and secure support for their children (DfE 2022). When I consider our systems in school, I mean the organisation: daily routines, the 'assess-plan-do-review', the writing and monitoring of support plans, the planning and classroom teaching, the internal process of the graduated response. I think that school-based systems should be straightforward. They are set out in policy. *However, if policy is not consistently used, then a policy is not worth the paper it is written on.*

In this chapter, I look closely at our policy and whole-school practice and argue that no matter how professionally written a policy is or how well it is followed, it is restricted in its effectiveness by the current climate. We cannot get away from the constrictions there are in funding, or the shortfall in NHS services and local authority specialists. This all impacts on staff practice, and as SENCO, I must be aware of what our team know and do, to ensure that our

SEND policy is followed and children receive high-quality teaching and support. Our school has been through a significant period of change, including a new build and COVID, and it was the organisation and consistent use of systems that had proved difficult to establish. Now ready to move forward, I decided that evaluating our SEND policy would be a key part of this process.

Collecting evidence to measure impact

Evidence collection

How much of our SEND policy does our staff access, know, understand and put into practice?

Discovering accurate knowledge of this would enable me to have a strategic, whole-school understanding of what influenced their practice. To collect this information, I carried out a whole-school questionnaire for all staff. This asked a range of questions covering whether they had read the policy, what they would do if they thought a child had SEND needs and about wider school practice.

I ensured that the questionnaire was anonymous and respected ethical boundaries. I have always believed that research has to have a purpose and provide learning. Yes, I intended to use the research to understand the impact of policy, but also wanted to collate thoughts and feelings. Participatory action research, as Kemmis et al. (2013) explain, works at its best when co-participants use a 'spiral' of self-reflection. By working in this way with colleagues, I intended to guide them to improve practice, so they could be wiser and more supportive in their classroom. By involving the voice of colleagues, I hoped to help them feel invested in the research and 'buy into whole-school change' to give our research a purpose.

Survey

The survey received 32 responses from the 93 sent out (see Table 10.1). There could be many reasons about the fact that only 33% of staff took part – change, lack of time or lack of interest. The results gave me something to consider, do staff know what our aims are or are they working based on their own perception of what is good provision? Are they being value-led or using experience?

Table 10.1 Breakdown of staff responses to survey

Staff role	Number of Surveys Sent	Number of Responses Received
	Total: 93 Sent	Total: 32 Responses
Teachers	30	19
Teaching Assistants	23	6
Midday Supervisors	23	2
Caretakers	2	0
Governors	10	5
Kitchen Staff	5	0

Impact

What do staff know, understand and do?

Of the 32 staff responding, 29 had read our SEND policy within the last year and 14 had read the SEND report. Some staff were clearly following processes described in our SEND policy, explaining how they carried out expected practices – for example, when asked 'What would you do if you think a child may need SEND support/may have special needs?' three replied:

> I begin by completing an initial concern form, then an assess-plan-review initially and then put some interventions in place for the individual concerned. If I am still concerned, I speak to the SENCO and request a meeting with parents about initial worries. We then arrange some formal observations to be carried out if parents agree.

> Initial concern form filled in and chat with SENCO, meet with parents to talk about concerns and plans to support, try to support in class with differentiated resources, grouping TA support, start to keep an assess-plan-review record, possible 'All about me' form for referral is needed, parent to sign for to agree to outside help.

> Carry out observation on the child, discuss with colleagues, talk to parents, talk to SENCO.

Others were not following the policy: eight (including a governor) said that they would refer this directly to the SENCO, while another seven said that they would talk to the class teacher/TA and the SENCO before doing anything themselves.

Several raised concerns about funding, either the lack of it or that external funding was delayed due to waiting for official diagnosis, which affected their practice:

> Not getting a diagnosis or support early enough so some children who clearly need one-to-one support don't receive funding for ages. Obviously, we do our best but it becomes more complicated if you are teaching a whole class on your own.

> Not having the time and resources to provide them with what they need. So many children who would receive additional support in an ideal world do not get the support they need because of lack of school budgets and external funding.

Other themes of concern about practice were raised by staff:

> The wide variety of issues covered by SEND inevitably means there are areas where I am inexperienced or have not come across a particular combination of needs.

> We can't help every child as some facts are not passed on.

> Some children appear to play the system without worries about serious repercussions.

> How children will cope with less support at secondary school.

> It is seen as the role of the TA or SENCO.

> The children who don't come under SEND but are struggling to access the curriculum and are falling behind.

Despite these concerns, staff were positive about the school's general response to meeting the needs of children with SEND, describing a wide range of successful inclusive practice:

> We know our children so well and therefore cater for their individual needs. We share information well so that all staff working with those children work consistently.

Coping with very severe physical and emotional needs – especially when other schools have given up on a child.

We make every effort to demonstrate that every child matters, we tailor lessons to allow all children to achieve success, no matter how big or small.

I feel we are very inclusive, children with SEND generally have their needs met to the best of our ability and we work hard to respond to any emotional needs. I think we have an ethos where all children are accepted and children without SEND understand why some children may have something additional/different.

We always aim to keep children in the classroom and involved in the same learning as everyone else, while adapting this learning to their needs.

Our relationship with parents and families and our continuing efforts to be inclusive in all aspects of school life.

Reflections and action

We need better communication – not all staff had current information about their class. I asked, did we know our children well enough? I identified through further conversations with staff that the issues were around children who were not on our SEND register. The information for key children was accurate and managed by myself. After the survey, I joined the general transition meetings with all year group teams, minuting and ensuring all information was correct and current. I emailed out minutes to teaching and assistant staff and produced a shortened version for office staff to provide to supply staff. I also asked that all SEND records are recorded on our online reporting system and correctly categorised. Review minutes, conversations about SEND and 'cause for concern' reports are all recorded there to create a clearer story of children's needs and provision.

With secondary transitions, I worked to ensure that shared spreadsheets requested were accurate; I introduced an online meeting held between the secondary school staff (tutors, year head, SENCO and pastoral staff) and our Year 6 teachers, myself and head teacher. Again, this is minuted, ensuring even the smallest piece of information or evidence is recorded to support smooth transition.

Children's challenging behaviour was a contentious issue. I needed to bring everyone along the journey to understanding, rationalising, and putting behaviours into context – to appreciate that behaviours are a way of communicating feelings children cannot articulate. The contentiousness often comes when adults want an immediate consequence or sanction. To address this, I worked with support from my head teacher to promote a member of our team to SLT with a TLR. I then have established a pastoral team led by myself, with the new behaviour and mental health lead and our senior teaching assistant. Together we have carried out a series of CPD sessions around the concept of trauma-informed practice. We have paid for an educational psychologist to deliver the initial part of this work. We have been vigilant about how we talk about behaviours in context with staff modelling appropriate language, with the expectation of embedding the practice. We have reviewed our behaviour policy, held parent meetings and presented our work to governors again building this ethos and approach.

It is possible that those who didn't read the policy hadn't done this because they felt it didn't have an impact on their daily work. We do share policies with staff at the beginning of every year and it is our expectation they are read, but this raises the question about how staff engage with such paperwork. For example, one of the issues subsequently discussed with governors was the number of complaints that come into school and how these are often SEN focussed. One governor spoke about parents' perceptions of the SENCO role. She explained that parents feel that if they have a SEN concern, I should be involved from the start. However, they should see their child's class teacher first. In a school as large as ours with 62 children at SEN support and 152 further children who are monitored (who may have diagnosis with Wave 1 or 2 provision), I need to be an advisor. Considering the Teaching Standard 5 (DFE 2011), it is a teacher's responsibility first and foremost to provide quality teaching for their pupils.

Reviewing the changes

To review the impact of our changes, we then asked the local authority to conduct a SEND audit of our provision. As part of a preparations audit, a second questionnaire was given to teachers and teaching assistants: 33 out of a possible 53 responded. As this was anonymous, I was unable to know if the respondents and/or their answers differed from those in the previous survey.

The results were generally very positive. In contrast to the earlier questionnaire, staff appeared confident in their awareness of individual needs. Communication between staff had improved, with 18 specifically mentioning the usefulness of previous teachers' transition information. Despite this, ten staff identified that the greatest risk to SEND provision was the state of external services and waiting times, and:

- 4 said they were not aware of the Code of Practice
- 7 did not know about the four broad areas of need
- 21 didn't know about the local authority offer
- 28 were not aware of the SEND information report
- 2 were not familiar with the SEND policy

This served as a reminder to me that however hard we try to engage everyone, some will not follow expected practice or access available information, so we must continue to audit this.

Recommendations

Recommendations for practice

The information collected from my research led to six key recommendations.

1. **Audit whole-school practice** – identify what everyone knows, understands and is doing. Don't assume that everyone has read your SEND policy and is following expected practice.
2. **Achieve a consistent approach across the whole school** – in a large school this is tricky, but with consistency in the use of policy comes confidence and understanding. Make sure all stakeholders understand your policy and involve them in the writing and review process. This was very powerful for us and really built a partnership.
3. **Quality First Teaching** – the best provision, support for all children: follow the assess, plan, do, review cycle and don't be afraid to ask for help from your colleagues. Senior leadership needs to monitor the quality of teaching and learning and this is a shared responsibility, whilst holding each other and the whole school team accountable.
4. **Training and continual CPD** – identify what your team needs, not just from what you see, but ask them – they will be then invested in this learning. For example, I knew from talking to the midday staff team's responses after their nonresponse to the original survey that they did not feel confident about their knowledge of autism, so I arranged training for them.

5. **Behaviour and SEND** – children's challenging behaviour is a contentious issue. Advising and training staff to deal with difficult behaviours raises issues with expectations. It is important to bring everyone along the journey to understanding, rationalising, and putting behaviours into contexts. This can be done with CPD sessions, reviewing behaviour policies, holding parent and governor meetings to build a supportive ethos.
6. **Awareness and sensitivity of the current climate and wellbeing** – this can be nationally, regionally or the climate of a family or household. Being sensitive to this gives you a better understanding and empathy when going into difficult conversations and meetings. This also gives you understanding about what they want, why they are asking the way they are asking.

Recommendations for leading whole-school development

Use the support of a SEND governor

Every term, I meet with our SEND governor. She has a great insight into views of the parents and the community. One such example is how the policy and local offer is written. She suggested rewriting it to make it accessible to parents, and explaining, for example, that the role of a SENCO is advisory and not teaching based. She argued that we needed to set out what parents' expectation should be and the role the family plays, and how we work in partnership. Encourage your SEND governor to share their expertise with other governors to overcome misunderstandings, like those identified about the SENCO role in our original survey.

Communication aids consistency

Using whole-school systems of recording is so vital, enabling everyone to access information shared and kept up to date. I use our school briefings to update staff on assessments of children taking place and also updates on key children. I want to nurture that collective responsibility.

One way I communicate with parents now is by holding termly coffee mornings for them with the pastoral team. Key individuals are invited to present about their role, like our mental health support team member and specialist teachers from the local authority.

This has been gratefully received. We also have a pastoral emailing list, with which we communicate support from services, information from charities, the local authority and health service. We also signpost to resources we share on our website. This has led to parents sharing slides from courses they have been on, showing they see the value of this way of working.

Be aware of mental health issues

I am raising mental health issues because it is not mentioned in our policy but was raised in our questionnaire answers. Families struggle against a culture that identifies difference in education. Dr Griffiths argues (2019), from his own personal experience, that persistent exclusionary approaches within education "draw attention to how disabled learners are problematised with the education system. If people are deemed 'special' then they can also be deemed a problem". This feeling of being a problem infiltrates every part of family life, for example repeated appointments at the doctors or repeated emails to school – they do not want to be 'that parent.' However, I would argue that in the current climate they can be nothing but 'that parent' to ensure their child receives the support they are entitled to.

Staying strong to your moral purpose

There may be policy, but we need to hold onto what drives our leadership – moral purpose, values and culture. I asked this question early on in this chapter. Managing and supporting families through challenges is part of my role. Our policy states that our objective is to 'work with parents/carers to gain a better understanding of their child and involve them in all stages of their child's education', which includes supporting their understanding of SEND procedures and practices, and providing termly opportunities to discuss provision and progress. This is not sufficient in the current climate and it is my moral purpose that pushes me to give families more. Parents and guardians increasingly ask for emotional support and last year, I completed a Royal Society for Public Health mental health first aid qualification. Families I see struggle with their child's behaviours and the impact that this has on their homelife and well-being.

In conclusion

As I stated earlier, the relationships I build with the children and their families is the aspect that rewards me most in my multiple roles. I also believe that the child should be at the centre of nearly every decision we make. We need to recognise the differences in our parents, staff, and pupils because

> The development of inclusive approaches to teaching and learning respect build on such differences. This may involve deep changes in what goes on in classrooms, staffrooms, playground and in relationships with parents/carers.
>
> (Booth and Ainscow 2016: 3–4)

Without these relationships, this deep understanding of each other and unconditional positive regard, we cannot work in a successful partnership, with or without policy. I believe the relationships I have and the belief in every child achieving their potential drives me to be the SENCO that I am. I am not perfect. As I stated at the beginning of this chapter, I do not believe that policy influences my daily work. I have highlighted inconsistencies in my own practice. I know that colleagues and governors hold me to account and may use policy to critique my effectiveness. Parents may use policy, the Code of Practice and legislation to ensure the school and I correctly support their child. However, I believe that without moral purpose and core principles, I would not challenge parents' views when I needed to, I would not challenge services that fall short and I certainly wouldn't keep striving in the current climate to ensure that all our pupils have the best teaching, provision and school experience we can possibly provide.

Recommended reading

Gross, J. (2023) *Beating Bureaucracy in Special Education Needs*. London: Routledge.
This provides useful discussions and practical help about how to manage SEN bureaucracy.

HM Government (2022) *SEND Review: Right Support Right Place Right Time*. London: HM Government. Available online at: www.gov.uk (Accessed 04/01/2024).
Yes, a government document, but a good place to refer to for key information.

Webster, R. (2022) *The Inclusion Illusion*. London: University College Press.
A really lovely thought-provoking book based on quality research. Webster argues that every teacher is a teacher of SEN.

References

Booth, T. and Ainscow, M. (2016) *Index for Inclusion: A Guide to School Development Led by Inclusive Values*. Cambridge: Index for Inclusion Network.

Curran, H., Heavey, A. and Boddison, A. (2018) *It's About Time: The Impact of SENCO Workload on the Professional and the School* [eBook]. Available online at: https://researchspace.bathspa.ac.uk/11859/bathspa.ac.uk (Accessed 04/01/2024).

Department for Education (2011) *Teachers' Standards Guidance for School Leaders, School Staff and Governing Bodies*. London: DFE. Available online at: https://assets.publishing.service.gov.uk/media/61b73d6c8fa8f50384489c9a/Teachers__Standards_Dec_2021.pdf (Accessed 12/07/2023).

Department for Education (2022) *SEND Review: Right Support Right Place Right Time*. London: Department for Education.

Department for Education and Department of Health (2015) *Special Educational Needs and Disability Code of Practice: 0–25 Years*. London: DfE and DoH.

Fullan, M. (2020) *Leading in a Culture of Change*, 2nd ed. Hoboken, NJ: Jossey-Bass [eBook]. Available online at: ebookcentral.proquest.com/lib/ntuuk/detail.action?docID=5990215&pq-origsite=primo (Accessed 04/01/2024).

Griffiths, M. (2019) *Current Debates: Part 1, Understanding Disability and the Problem with "Special"*. London: Alliance for Inclusive Education. Available online at: https://www.allfie.org.uk/resources/item/page/2/. (Accessed 24/07/2023).

Kemmis, S., McTaggart, R. and Nixon, R. (2013) *The Action Research Planner: Doing Critical Participatory Action Research*. Singapore: Springer.

Index

Note: Page numbers in *italics* indicate a figure and page numbers in **bold** indicate a table on the corresponding page.

Printed in the United States
by Baker & Taylor Publisher Services